THE REMINISCENCES OF

Mr. Jesse W. Arbor
Member of the Golden Thirteen

INTERVIEWED BY

Paul Stillwell

U.S. Naval Institute • Annapolis, Maryland

Copyright © 2018

Preface

In the late 1980s I set out to interview the eight then-living members of the first 13 African American line officers commissioned by the U.S. Navy. They had gone through a short training course in 1944. After the process of going around the circuit to do the interviews, I found myself much better informed about the group, which had acquired the sobriquet "The Golden Thirteen" retroactively. I found myself wishing I'd been that knowledgeable about them when I started. In addition, I had provided copies of each man's interview transcript to the other seven members of the group still living. Then I decided to go around and conduct a second round of interviews with all eight. This time I was able to ask questions out of a wider background of knowledge, and I discovered an unexpected bonus. By the second time around, the men had concluded that my motives were sincere, and some of them opened up more candidly than they had the first time.

Jesse Arbor was a pleasure to work with, in part because he was so entertaining. But that was also a drawback. As Arbor himself put it in one interview, "I may be a little frivolous at times, which is part of my makeup. It is part of my game plan." That game plan was useful when the officer candidates were going through training at Great Lakes Naval Training Station. The pace of learning was compressed and demanding, sometimes leading to men getting on each other's nerves. Arbor had a gift for throwing in a joke or some other observation that lightened the atmosphere. The drawback, as far as history is concerned, is that his frivolity included exaggeration and a tendency to relate some of his recollections with tongue in cheek. As his cohorts put it, "That's just Jesse."

So the reader should bear in mind that the memoir that follows is not always the literal truth. Sometimes the exaggerations are obvious, but not always. What does come through clearly is that Arbor was sincere in his desire to do his best for the Navy, to master it professionally, and to serve as a mentor for those coming along after he left active duty. He took great pride in performing well in the essence of the naval profession—serving on board ships at sea. Ironically, though the men of the Golden Thirteen were trained in the skills of operating ships, the racial climate of the time prevented all but a few from serving sea duty as commissioned officers. Arbor's sea service was entirely as an enlisted man. He felt a great sense of honor at being able to serve as a role model and inspiration for younger generations.

For a variety of reasons, the completion of this project has taken far longer than it should have. One factor was that the initial transcriber had a difficult time understanding many of the spoken words. A second transcription provided a considerably more accurate rendition, though the text at times contains the notation "unclear" for things that could still not be deciphered. Even so, the transcript captures Arbor's energetic spirit and a good deal of his philosophy for living in a world in which people are too often judged initially by the color of their skin.

For their roles in collecting and preserving oral recollections, I am grateful for the support of Janis Jorgensen and Eric Mills of the Naval Institute staff. Susan Corrado of the Naval Institute Press has coordinated the printing and binding of the finished product.

In completing this volume, the Naval Institute expresses its gratitude to the Tawani Foundation and the Pritzker Military Library of Chicago for their generous financial support of the oral history program that produced this memoir.

Paul Stillwell
U.S. Naval Institute
April 2018

The U.S. Naval Institute Oral History Program

Researchers and authors have been drawing on the Naval Institute's Oral History Program since 1969, the year it was established by Dr. John T. Mason Jr. He and his successor, author and historian Paul Stillwell, sought to capture, preserve, and disseminate a permanent record of the stories of significant figures in naval history. Under the leadership of Vice Adm. Peter H. Daly, U.S. Navy (Ret.), CEO of the Institute, the program has expanded, with increasing numbers of historians conducting more interviews.

These oral histories are carefully fact-checked and reviewed by both historians and interview subjects before being made available. The Naval Institute is known for this high level of editorial intervention and polishing. The reader is reminded, as with all oral history interviews, that this is a record of the spoken word.

The Naval Institute wishes to acknowledge the many donors who make this program possible, in particular the generous support of the Pritzker Military Foundation of Chicago and the late Jack C. Taylor of St. Louis.

JESSE WALTER ARBOR
MEMBER OF THE GOLDEN THIRTEEN

Jesse Walter Arbor was born 26 December 1914 in Cotton Plant, Arkansas, one of 12 children of Tecora and Alexander Arbor. He had two sisters and nine brothers. He grew up in the rural town of Cotton Plant, which was essentially all black. His ancestors had received land in the area when slavery ended. Outgoing and loquacious by nature, Arbor also had a tendency to joke and exaggerate concerning his life history. During an oral history interview he described Cotton plant as, "A little place that only me and the Good Lord knows [with a population of] 1,661 up until the day I left, and there's never been that many since."

As with his siblings, Arbor received a private school education. During his years in Arkansas he attended Arkadelphia-Cotton Plant Academy. Around 1930 the family left the farm area and moved to Chicago as part of a northerly migration of blacks seeking employment opportunities. Arbor's father worked as a carpenter, and his children attended Catholic schools. Because of his athletic prowess, several colleges sought to recruit Arbor in the early 1930s. He accepted a football scholarship at an all-black school, Arkansas Agricultural, Mechanical & Normal (AM&N) College, now the University of Arkansas at Pine Bluff. A large, solidly built man, Arbor played right tackle on the football team and majored in the social sciences. He left school one semester short of a degree, after his football eligibility expired.

In 1935 Arbor observed that black professionals were not well paid, so he returned to Illinois and took a job at the Chicago Beach Hotel as doorman and receiving clerk. As he explained, he preferred pay to prestige. In 1939 he became a Pullman porter on trains that traveled widely about the country, then returned to Chicago to become a tailor. The United States entered World War II in December 1941, and Arbor enlisted in the Navy in September 1942—shortly before he would have been drafted into the Army. He went through recruit training at all-black Camp Robert Smalls, part of the large naval training station complex at Great Lakes, Illinois, north of Chicago.

As a sailor, Arbor advanced to quartermaster second class; the quartermaster rating was involved with navigation, logkeeping, and visual signaling. He was among the first blacks rated in that specialty. Arbor was initially stationed in the Boston area, where he served on board two coastal minesweepers and took an advanced navigation course in a Navy facility at Harvard University. In late 1943 Arbor's life changed dramatically when he was ordered to report back to Camp Robert Smalls to take part in the Navy's first officer training course for African Americans.

Of the approximately one hundred thousand black sailors then in the Navy, Arbor and fifteen other men were chosen to begin the training in January 1944. The service-wide selection process included FBI background checks and recommendations on leadership ability. Amost all in the group had college experience, and a few had advanced degrees. In two and a half months, they went through a cram course that included training in such areas as navigation, communications, gunnery, propulsion machinery, seamanship, naval history, and the Navy disciplinary system. It essentially involved a great deal of memory work, for which Arbor was well suited.

The members of the training class concluded that they were part of an experiment on the part of the Navy and determined to succeed or fail as a group, rather than compete with each other. Thus they pooled their knowledge in after-hours sessions. The men were not only in segregated Camp Robert Smalls but also separated from all other black trainees. At times the constant togetherness and the novelty of much of the material led to frayed nerves. Arbor and Dennis Nelson, one of the other officer candidates, often defused the tension with humor. The group did exceptionally well in exams. All sixteen passed the course in March 1944, but the Navy chose to commission Arbor and eleven others as ensigns; one man in the course, Charles Lear, became a warrant officer. The other three remained as enlisted men. Years later the pioneer officers received a distinctive group identity when they were retroactively named the "Golden Thirteen."

Once they became officers, Arbor and Lear received assignments to the supply depot in Pearl Harbor, Hawaii; they were the first two black naval officers to be assigned overseas. The executive officer of the depot paved the way for their arrival by specifying that they should be treated with respect and no discrimination. Among his duties, Arbor was at times assigned as shore patrol officer and delighted in wearing a .45-caliber automatic pistol on his hip as a badge of authority. Subsequently Arbor and Lear transferred to the island of Guam, which was gearing up for the planned invasion of Japan in 1945. The two served as troubleshooters in supply and logistics. As the senior black officer in the area, Arbor also served essentially as an unofficial advisor for black sailors.

Once the war was over, Arbor left the service and returned to Chicago's south side, where he resumed his work in the clothing business. He set up his own dry cleaning and tailor shop and in 1948 married Autry Brown. They had three children: Jesse Jr., Deborah and Brenda. Arbor's work in his shop continued until 1968, when a combination of urban renewal and concerns about his health led him to seek other employment. He applied to the Chicago board of education and was asked what he could do. As he did so often in life, Arbor gave a flip answer: "Run my mouth and boss like hell." He took a job running heating systems in various schools and performing administrative duties. He finally retired in 1984 at age seventy. In the years after that he aided Navy recruiting of minorities and met with later generations of black naval officers. He summed up his achievements by saying of the Golden Thirteen: "Having been one of the guinea pigs, I'm glad I had the endurance and fortitude to withstand the challenges we faced. . . . The black officers today express their appreciation when they see us."

Mr. Arbor died on 11 January 2000.

Deed of Gift

The U.S. Naval Institute is hereby authorized to make available in any format it chooses, from bound-book hard copy to electronic/digital Internet access and as part of videorecordings, the audio recordings, transcripts, and videorecordings of the oral-history interview series conducted concerning the life and career of the late Jesse W. Arbor. Disposition, repositories, and access shall be at the discretion of the Naval Institute.

The undersigned does hereby release and assign to the U.S. Naval Institute the rights and title to these interviews, with the exception that the undersigned and heirs retain the right to use the material for personal, noncommercial purposes. The copyright in the oral, transcribed, and videorecorded versions shall be held by the U.S. Naval Institute. All recordings, transcriptions, and videorecordings of the interviews shall remain the property of the U.S. Naval Institute.

Signed and sealed this __21__ day of __May__ 2018.

Signed name __Autry Arbor__
Printed name __Autry Arbor__

Interview Number 1 with Mr. Jesse W. Arbor, member of the Golden Thirteen
Place: Mr. Arbor's home in Chicago, Illinois
Date: Thursday, 9 October 1986

Mr. Arbor: This tape should have been taken as far back as, I'll say, 1948 or '49. Since that time, I'm an old man now, and senility has already set in.

Paul Stillwell: No, I don't think so.

Mr. Arbor: My memory is a little befuddled now. I didn't know who recommended me when I came back to Great Lakes.*

Paul Stillwell: How did you get into the Navy in the first place?

Mr. Arbor: Ducking the Army. I had three brothers who were already in the Army. They told me, "Go anywhere you can go other than this place. Don't come." So when I got my "welcome" to come in the Army, I went over there to Lake Park and drew $500.00 out of the Hyde Park Bank. I went down to Mexico City and stayed 30 days. When I got busted, I came back and looked in my mailbox at all those brown envelopes. That Saturday morning, I broke out and went downtown on Plymouth Court and joined the Navy.

Paul Stillwell: What was the purpose of your 30-day hiding out?

Mr. Arbor: I didn't intend to come back.

Paul Stillwell: Oh, I see.

---

* From January to March 1944, 16 black Navy enlisted men received officer training in a special program at Camp Robert Smalls, part of the naval training station at Great Lakes, Illinois, north of Chicago. Arbor was one of the 16; 13 of the 16 became officers in March 1944.

Mr. Arbor: I was young and crazy. The war was on. I heard Roosevelt make that declaration of war.* I was sitting at 12th Street there, waiting for the 12th Street store to open up so I could buy me a new suit. I didn't buy the suit. First, I had bought a brand-new '40 Plymouth and just gotten out of school. I remembered my mother's brothers coming home from World War I and how they talked about how rough it was in France, and all like that. All I wanted to do was duck the Army and learn how to smoke cigars like my uncle, because they smelled so good, those good cigars. They looked so good in a uniform. So I went down to the recruiting station that Saturday morning.

Paul Stillwell: When would this be now?

Mr. Arbor: That was in early September 1942. When I walked in the recruiting office at 11:30, the yeoman was putting on his dress jumper, fixing to go. He said, "What do you want, Mac?"

I said, "I want to join the Navy."

"Come back Monday. I'm going on liberty."

I said, "Can't you get—?"

He said, "Come back Monday, Mac." So he started on out the door.

There was a jaygee in there putting on his coat.† He said, "Jess, what are you doing here?" It was somebody I knew.

Paul Stillwell: Who was that?

Mr. Arbor: That was the recruiting officer who was in charge of all of naval recruiting down on Plymouth Court. I told him, "Mr. Weaver, I've got to get in the Navy today."

He said, "What?" I showed him the letter. So he called the yeoman back and said, "Let's take his name, date it as of today." He said me, "You be here first thing Monday morning, and we'll swear you in." That's how I got in the Navy. The yeoman

---

* On Sunday, 7 December 1941, Japanese carrier planes attacked and heavily damaged American warships at the naval base at Pearl Harbor, Hawaii. The U.S. Congress declared war on Japan the next day after hearing President Franklin D. Roosevelt make an address.
† Jaygee – lieutenant (junior grade).

was so mad, he typed—I had three different numbers. I had one on my pay voucher, ID card, and a different one for the dog tags. It took about six months to get me straightened out.

Then, after I got in the Navy, I was there 30 days, and then the FBI came up.[*] They wanted to get me out of the Navy and charge me for draft evasion. They said, "How are you going to charge him for draft evasion? He's in the Navy." So I ducked that rap.

I finished boot camp.[†] They gave us, I think, 10 or 12 days' leave. I came back and made service school. I went through service school and came out as quartermaster third class.[‡]

Paul Stillwell: Where did you go to service school?

Mr. Arbor: Great Lakes. After service school, they sent me to the receiving station there in Boston. I was there two days, and they sent me over to Pier One in East Boston. They didn't know what to do with rated seamen.[§] They couldn't put us in the kitchen, so they didn't know what to do with us. So, finally, they started putting us on those minesweepers and harbor craft. After they found out that I knew semaphore and flashing lights, could read those good, they put me on the docks directing those British ships and Australian ships in to the docks.

Paul Stillwell: Did you know Sublett?[**] He was there too.

---

[*] FBI – Federal Bureau of Investigation.
[†] "Boot" is a slang term for a newly enlisted sailor or Marine. Recruit training is known as boot camp. For Arbor it was in the same segregated Camp Robert Smalls where he received his officer training in 1944.
[‡] Quartermaster is a Navy enlisted rating that specializes in navigation. Third class is pay grade E-4, the most junior of the petty officers.
[§] On 7 April 1942 the Navy agreed to accept black sailors into general service ratings as of 1 June of that year. That change meant an opportunity to go into a range of different occupational specialties, rather than being confined largely to duties as cooks, stewards, and messmen.
[**] Frank Ellis Sublett Jr. was a member of the Golden Thirteen. His oral history is in the Naval Institute collection.

Mr. Arbor: I didn't know Sublett until we came back—I didn't know any of these boys until we all reassembled and the Navy sent us back to Great Lakes. Sublett went through service school down at Hampton Institute.*

Paul Stillwell: Right. He was a motor machinist's mate.

Mr. Arbor: The only two that knew each other were Judge White and Lewis Reginald Williams, who didn't make it, because they had gone to school at the University of Chicago.†

I was called off the docks one day to go aboard a minesweeper as a quartermaster third class. After being out there about six weeks or two months, I was then transferred to an advanced course in navigation at Dutton Hall at Harvard University there at Boston. After I had completed that course, I came out as quartermaster second class. They sent me back to sea on a little larger ship then.

Paul Stillwell: What was that?

Mr. Arbor: That was a minesweeper, but it was a bigger one. It was seaworthy. We would just go out today and come back tomorrow, like that little one I was on. I was on the bigger one, I'd say, about two months.

They made a mistake and had that air raid system hooked up all over Boston. One day they announced that they were going to commission a destroyer escort, the *Mason*, and going to put on an all-colored crew.‡ That was the thing they used in those days. They didn't use the word "black;" it was "colored." An all-colored crew on there, and my name was the first name called to go aboard. They made a mistake and didn't

---

* Commander Edwin H. Downes, USNR, was a Naval Academy graduate who had resigned his commission, worked in the field of education, and then been recalled to active service for World War II. He was officer in charge of the Naval Training School at Hampton, Virginia. He recommended some of the enlisted men at Hampton for inclusion in this first officer training program.

† William Sylvester White was a member of the Golden Thirteen. His oral history is in the Naval Institute collection. His friend Lewis R. "Mummy" Williams was one of the three officer candidates who went through the training program but did not become officers.

‡ USS *Mason* (DE-529), an *Evarts*-class destroyer escort, was commissioned 20 March 1944. The ship's officers were white; the enlisted men were black.

disconnect the citywide air raid, so my name went all over Boston. Boy, my chest flew wide open. I lashed up my seabag, went down to board it. They put on my buddy, a third class, instead and told me, "No, Arbor, you can't go." They didn't tell me any reason why. This was November 1943. I got so mad I didn't know what to do. I just sat down. I didn't do enough to get court-martialed.

Paul Stillwell: You expressed your discontent.

Mr. Arbor: So they sent me to another class that was supposed to start January first, back to Harvard. So I felt, "What the hell? "Can't do anything now. I'm in the Navy. I've been in the Navy long enough to know you do what you're told; never volunteer."

So after Christmas leave in Chicago, I went back to Boston a little before the first of January, and I'd been gone almost 30 days. I came back here and ran around. When I got back there, everything I had was dirty, so I took it off and threw it in the washing machine—peacoat, everything, because everything was filthy. I was an enlisted man, and a lot of this stuff is not good for the record. I went back there, and they had a little poker game going back then. I was broke, and I hadn't been there for two paydays, so I borrowed some money. I just had left the CO's office, checking in. About the time I got in the poker game, somebody came up and said, "Jesse Arbor, quartermaster second class, report to officer of the deck."

I said, "Hell, I just left there." I looked up. Wasn't no officer supposed to be up on the second deck. I looked up, and there was a full commander.

He said, "Next case."

I said, "Sir, I don't have anything to put on." It was cold now, in January, so I was sitting down in my skivvy shirt and shorts, playing poker. I said, "In 35 minutes, it will all be out of the washing machine, and I've got to dry something." There wasn't but two guys in the barracks my size.

So he said, "I'll go back over and tell them."

I went back down. Before I could get my hand dealt out, somebody else ran up the steps. "Jesse Arbor, you're wanted by the officer of the deck on the double."

I looked up, and there was a captain. I said, "Goddamn!"

Paul Stillwell: That was a tough poker game.

Mr. Arbor: So I reached over to a boy and said, "Give me a pair of pants." I looked over, and there was a peacoat. I started down the steps, and when I got down to the bottom of the steps, there was another captain, and he had a brown envelope.

He said, "You got ten minutes to get your seabag lashed up. There's a car sitting downstairs there to take you to the Back Bay Station. In 35 minutes, you're going back to Chicago."

Hell, I just left. I got to thinking. I had wrecked a Packard for a doctor right on the corner of 51st and South Park. I had an old Pontiac I was driving. I thought, "They're sending me back there for that accident." I jumped in the car, got on the train.

Paul Stillwell: Did you collect your clothes in the meantime?

Mr. Arbor: No, I couldn't, because the machine hadn't quit. I just kept that boy's peacoat, and that's all I had. They told me, "We'll send them to you. Go ahead." So I got off downtown at Union Station, and a sailor was there, looking for me.

Paul Stillwell: Did you even have a jumper on?

Mr. Arbor: Yes, I had an undress jumper and a peacoat that wasn't quite my size. Nothing fitted me, because nothing was mine but my shoes and socks.

They rushed me right up to Great Lakes that Monday. I got there around 1:00 o'clock, and they rushed me right on over to a warm barracks. Two or three guys were sitting around. That night, all 16 of us were there.

Paul Stillwell: Did you know what you were there for?

Mr. Arbor: No! Because when they passed that envelope in, they took it. On the top deck, there were 16 bunks, 16 chairs, and two of those long chow hall tables drawn together. On the first deck of the building, there was one entire barracks, upper and lower, there were 16 chairs, one desk, looked like an improvised library around there. So I just thought I was back in another service school. I had been in and out of service schools. So did Sublett and the rest of them.

Paul Stillwell: At least you weren't getting prosecuted for the accident.

Mr. Arbor: No. That was off my mind. Nelson was the last one to get there.* Now Nelson's father and grandfather had been in the Navy, one in the Civil War, one in World War I, and all like that. All of them were firemen or something like that—never worked in the kitchen. Nelson was the only man in the Navy who had a cape, other than President Roosevelt at that time, and he flaunted it. He knew naval procedure from just talking to his father and old sea stories from his grandfather. He remembered his grandfather and all that kind of stuff.

We stayed in that class, I guess, four weeks.

Paul Stillwell: What did that cover?

Mr. Arbor: That covered, "Now if you were—these were the things that officers learn." They didn't tell us we were in officers' candidate school, but we were kept void of contact from anyone, excepting ourselves, all day long. We had to go to the chow hall, march by ourselves, and go before anybody else ate.

Paul Stillwell: Did you march to chow?

Mr. Arbor: We marched to chow, they marched us back, right back in that barracks. No weekend leaves or nothing.† Eight hours' classroom work every day.

Paul Stillwell: What were you studying?

---

* Dennis Denmark Nelson II was one of the Golden Thirteen.
† The men did get at least some weekends off.

Mr. Arbor: Navy regs, naval law, math, history, science, economics—just the same things you take in a college.

Paul Stillwell: How much education did you have at that point?

Mr. Arbor: Three years and six months in college.

Paul Stillwell: What school had you gone to?

Mr. Arbor: Arkansas State College and Lewis Institute.[*] Before it was IIT here, it was Lewis Institute on the west side.[†] Everybody in this officer-training class—there were five master's degrees, two high school graduates, and three of us were juniors in college. I needed three more months.

Paul Stillwell: Why had you not completed your degree at that point?

Mr. Arbor: The last year in college, I had played out my eligibility in football, so I would have to go the following year, and I didn't have $38.00 to pay for that semester, so I had to go.

Paul Stillwell: Where had your home been?

Mr. Arbor: Here.

Paul Stillwell: How did you wind up at Arkansas?

Mr. Arbor: Well, now, I had a choice. I would have gone to Clark College in Atlanta, but I couldn't get my railroad fare. I had a scholarship to Wilberforce in Ohio; I couldn't get my fare there. I had six or seven scholarships, but I couldn't get the bus fare there.

---
[*] The institution is now the University of Arkansas at Pine Bluff; during Arbor's time as a student it was Arkansas Agricultural, Mechanical and Normal (AM&N) College.
[†] IIT – Illinois Institute of Technology.

So the coach from Arkansas State College was over in Gary recruiting.* He heard about me some kind of way, and he came over and found me and took me back. That's how I got there.

Getting back to this class, we had been in that class for four or six weeks, and I was beginning to get tired of that sh—"If you were—" Everything was subjunctive. So Big Barnes, who is dead now, Phil Barnes, P. G. Barnes, got close to me.† Sublett was living in Evanston then, and Syl and Williams and I were the only ones who lived in Chicago. The rest of the boys were from out of the city. I had gotten my car up to Great Lakes, so if we got a leave, I could come home. So Big Barnes sat next to me—A, B—so we became close friends.

One Saturday, he got a card from his baby sister out in Washington, D.C., and she said, "Little brother, here's my phone number where I want you to call me, and you give me a phone number where I can call you next Saturday, and tell me what time."

He wrote to her, and she called him about 4:00 o'clock that following Saturday. It was the first leave we'd had, and as we were coming down, the phone rang. He was close to the phone. I said, "Get it, big boy." He got it, and it was his little baby sister.

She said, "Little brother, something's going on funny here." She was the chambermaid for the Secretary of the Navy Forrestal at that time.‡ She said, "I see a list of men here that they're going to be some kind of officers."

He said, "What?"

"Don't tell anybody now, because it's top secret, and it's not supposed to be on this desk. I can't pick it up, but I can read. It doesn't say what date it's going to be, but they're going to make the first colored officers."

He said, "Read that list there."

She said, "Jesse Arbor, Phil Barnes, Dalton Baugh," she went on alphabetically.§

---

* Gary, Indiana, is near Chicago.
† Phillip George Barnes and Samuel Edward Barnes were both members of the Golden Thirteen. The oral history of Samuel Barnes is in the Naval Institute collection; Phillip Barnes died before he could be interviewed.
‡ James V. Forrestal served as Under Secretary of the Navy from 22 August 1940 to 16 May 1944. He became Secretary of the Navy on 19 May, following the death of Frank Knox, who was Secretary at the time the Golden Thirteen members were in officer training.
§ Dalton Louis Baugh was a member of the Golden Thirteen. He died before he could be interviewed by the Naval Institute's oral history program.

He said, "What is the rank they're going to get?"

She said, "En-signs or something."

So he said, "Are you kidding?"

She said, "No, that's what I see right on this paper." So we went back upstairs, and he told me what was going on. So we got in the car, came on over here.

I knew one person in Boston that everywhere I turned, that officer was either looking over my shoulder, or his name was on my leave papers, but he wasn't in charge of me. He was a naval captain from the deck, got his legs shot off in World War I.

Paul Stillwell: What was his name, do you know?

Mr. Arbor: Charles E.—or Charles M.—Bamford.* That Monday night when I came back, it just worried me. I said, "I'm going to call Boston." I knew what time to call him after he would be through eating his dinner at night. So I called him in Boston that Monday night, and I said, "Captain Bamford?"

"Yes?"

I said, "This is Quartermaster Second Class Arbor."

"Yes. How are you getting along, boy?"

I said, "Sir, I don't know. I'm so tired of this sh—if you were—these are the things one should know if one were to become—"

He said, "Wait a minute, boy. You go back in that classroom, keep your damn mouth shut and your nose clean. Nobody in the Ninth Naval District can help you nor hurt you. That little fellow Armstrong, the commander in charge of the program—he's supposed to know just how and why every colored person was born and what he was born for.† That little fellow can't help you nor hurt you." I hadn't even called his name.

---

* In the officer registers of the period, the person who most closely fits this description is Robert T. Bamford, who retired as a lieutenant (junior grade) in 1920. He was promoted to lieutenant on the retired list in May 1943. He was then nearly 50 years old and lived in Ipswich, Massachusetts.

† Commander Daniel W. Armstrong, USNR, was officer in charge of Camp Robert Smalls. He was a 1915 Naval Academy graduate who resigned his regular commission after World War I and was recalled to active duty for World War II, serving at Great Lakes and in the Pacific theater. Daniel Armstrong (1893-1947) was the son of Samuel Chapman Armstrong, founder of Hampton Institute in Virginia. He was born the same year his father died.

I said, "Thank you, sir." So I went back and told Barnes what Captain Bamford had said. So we went on back to class there and were a little relieved. They didn't tell us up until the day—as I say, I wish this had been taken years ago, where it would have been fresh on my mind—up until the day they told us to fall out in columns of—

[Telephone interruption]

Mr. Arbor: I forget where I left off.

Paul Stillwell: You were talking about coming back to class after you'd talked to Captain Bamford.

Mr. Arbor: Yes. When we received the commission, they told us to fall out of the barracks in columns of two. Well, now that was unusual, because we had been to breakfast, and it wasn't early enough for noon chow. This was around 10:00 o'clock. So we came down, out of the barracks, and some guy was standing out there. We didn't know we were being photographed. That's when Pathé News used to come on in all these moving picture theaters.

Paul Stillwell: Newsreels.

Mr. Arbor: Newsreels. They said, "One go this direction, every other one go that direction." So we were just walking. We walked all the way around the square and came back, and went upstairs.

Paul Stillwell: Were you still wearing enlisted uniforms?

Mr. Arbor: Yes. All of us had been elevated to first class then, except Nelson and Cooper; they came in the Navy as chief recruiters, so they were wearing chiefs' uniforms.* The rest of us had on first class stripes. Barnes, Baugh, and myself were the only ones who had right-arm ratings.† All the rest of them had left-arm ratings. But they were below deck—firemen, motor machs, or something, and we were either boatswains or quartermasters or signalmen.

We went back upstairs, and the next morning, they told us, "Go to the battalion commander's office." One by one, they gave us our commissions like that. No formal graduation exercise, no anything. Here was our commission, and they told us, "Go over to main side and get fitted out for a uniform."‡

I shall never forget Armstrong. He said, "You're Arbor."

I said, "Yes, sir."

"How did you get here?"

I said, "Sir, I don't know."

"You mean to tell me you don't know?" I was the only one he didn't have anything to do with, other than Pinkney, Alves—we were the only ones, as I remember, that he didn't have something in hand in picking us.§ So his first remarks to me were, "Now that you're an officer, how do you feel?"

I said, "Sir, having never been an officer before, didn't have an idea that's what I was in school for, I will first have to be an officer a day or two before I know how I feel."

He said, "I understand all of you made good grades over there, and that's commendable. Now you know you will have to make choices as an officer instead of an enlisted man."

---

* George Clinton Cooper was a member of the Golden Thirteen. His oral history is in the Naval Institute collection. Prior to commissioning, Nelson was a petty officer first class; Cooper was the only chief petty officer in the group.

† Before and during World War II, some enlisted men in the Navy's seagoing specialties were distinguished by wearing their rating badges on the right sleeves of their uniform jumpers. Included were such ratings as boatswain's mate, mineman, quartermaster, signalman, gunner's mate, turret captain, torpedoman's mate, and fire controlman. Petty officers in the other ratings wore the insignia on their left sleeves.

‡ The "main side" of the Great Lakes training station contained the administrative offices. It was separate from Camp Robert Smalls, the site of training for black sailors.

§ J. B. Pinkney, A. Alves, and Lewis Reginald "Mummy" Williams were the three members of the 16 candidates who did not become officers. Bernard C. Nalty, *Strength for the Fight* (New York: The Free Press, 1986), makes the following statement on page 192: ". . . on January 1, 1944, sixteen black enlisted men entered a segregated officer candidate school at the Great Lakes Naval Training Station. Although all of them successfully completed the course, only twelve received commissions, a purely arbitrary number adopted by the Bureau of Personnel for reasons never explained. Of the remaining four, one became a warrant officer, and the others reverted to enlisted status."

I said, "Yes, sir."

He said, "Now, in the event that you would be in a position where there was a colored sailor and a white sailor in a fight, whose side would you take?"

I said, "Sir, I have to wait until that occasion arises." He looked at me. I said, "The first thing I would think of to do is as an officer, as has been taught to me. It's the only thing I could rely on. My personal judgment would not enter into the case."

He reared back. He said, "Well, that sounds pretty good. Now I want to tell you." He took the orders and read it on there. I've got it somewhere. "Now you know there are no quarters for you in the BOQ."*

I said, "I didn't know that. Our instructions were in class of the duties, the obligations."

The second thing he said was, "I don't want any of you fellows going to the officers' club."

So the first orders I got, after I got my commission, I stayed there. Then they gave us ten days to go on leave before we got our assignment. So Baugh and I went back to Arkansas State College, because after we got our commission, all these boys, excepting Dalton Baugh, myself, Pinkney, Alves, and Nelson, were from Big Ten colleges. So all those buzzards wanted to know, "How did two little guys like you all from a little no-name college, two out of 13, get commissioned?" They razzed us up and down.

So Baugh said, "Jess, let's go back to Arkansas State College."

Paul Stillwell: Who was razzing you, the Big Ten guys?

Mr. Arbor: Yes, all the rest of them. When Mummy Williams didn't make it, from Chicago University, "Where is Arkansas?" The saddest disappointment I had up until that time—we went back to Arkansas State College; Baugh and I went on the campus. Now, the dean of the college at that time was one of my classmates and Baugh's classmates. He didn't have time to talk to us. I have been invited to about 20 or 25 different colleges and universities, to speak to different clubs and things like that since

---

* BOQ – bachelor officers' quarters.

then. I've never been asked to come back to Arkansas State College up until the last year, after Baugh died, and I had been down there three times since then.* I'd been through there and stopped by there, and the dean had been elevated to the president of the college at one time. When Baugh died, he wanted to give us some recognition. I told him, "To hell with you," and I haven't been down since.

But after I left Great Lakes, after we had our leave, 10 or 12 days, whatever it was, after we got our commission, Boatswain Lear and I were the first ones they sent overseas.† They sent us to Pearl Harbor. When I got to Pearl Harbor—I wasn't supposed to see it, but Ensign Kidd, from Portland, Oregon, or either Joe Hise, one of them, saved it. After I was there about four or five days, he slipped it to me. I've tried to keep some of those things that I thought you would be interested in and pulled them from the files. All those cabinets over there are full of that kind of stuff. The memo was to the effect that there were black officers in the Navy.

Paul Stillwell: Who was it from and who was it to?

Mr. Arbor: Secretary of the Navy to all officers of the United States Navy. There it is.

Paul Stillwell: This is from Lieutenant Commander, Supply Corps, USN, S. B. McCune. He was executive officer of the naval supply depot, and it's dated 21 February 1945. It's a memorandum to all officers. "Subject: Negro officers. 1. There are now attached to this depot two Negro officers. Their services are sorely needed by the naval supply depot, and they were therefore requested by the supply officer in command. 2. These officers are to be given the same respect as any other officer in the U.S. Navy. They will be quartered and messed in regular quarters and mess halls in this depot. 3. No discrimination of any kind will be shown these officers, and they will be treated equally with all other officers. Any officer violating this order will be sternly dealt with."

---

* Baugh died in 1985, the year before this interview took place.
† Charles Byrd Lear was a member of the Golden Thirteen. He became a boatswain, that is, a warrant officer, in March 1944. The other 12 were commissioned as ensigns.

Paul Stillwell: Did that wind up helping you?

Mr. Arbor: It did. I'm almost sure it did, because every officer all over the Pacific got one of them. I wish I had had a videotape and a recording device to have taped some of those conversations and questions that were asked of me and Lear when we first got out there. They wanted to know why you were born, where, what for. Just any kind of simple question. I've walked in many officers' clubs out in the Pacific, and some of them evidently hadn't heard of it. They'd be drinking, and I've seen them bite plugs out of a glass and turn around. Some of them had on Bermuda shorts. Once you hit Pearl Harbor all the way out, every officer had a .45. They'd look up and see me, everywhere I'd go. See, all the whiskey was free out there. You didn't buy any whiskey out there. It was rationed. You'd get two quarts of whiskey and one quart of Scotch, one rum, one lime to take to your quarters once a month. But when you'd go to the officers' club, all you'd do is set your glass up there. You didn't have to pay for anything there. You didn't have to pay for what you took away. They wondered why could I drink so much whiskey and never get drunk. Officers were getting drunk, falling over, and I'd have to take them to the BOQ and all like that.

I didn't realize that I was being tailed by the Secret Service. Lear and I were tailed. They hadn't sent anybody else overseas but Lear and I.

Paul Stillwell: Do you know why you got sent over there?

Mr. Arbor: Alphabetical. That's the way we figured everything came up, by my name being Arbor. If it was good, I got it first. If it was bad, I got it first.

Paul Stillwell: Lear's not alphabetically . . .

Mr. Arbor: But he was the only warrant officer, so they sent him along so I'd have a companion. That's all I can say it was. I never shall forget when we left for Pearl Harbor, went over to Kwajalein, and I was supposed to have gone down to the Marianas Islands, to New Hebrides, to pick up a bunch of sailors and bring them back to Guam, but some way the orders got mixed up, so they sent me directly to Guam. When I got to Guam, Lear came over. I went down to the officers' club that night with little Joe Hise, a little ensign from Rome, Georgia, a little Jewish boy. He said, "Man, oh man, oh man. This is going to be a party in itself."

I said, "What is that, Joe?"

He said, "A black and a Jew going to the officers' club. Neither one of us is wanted."

I said, "To hell with what they want now. The war is on now. I didn't ask to come over here. You give me a damn ticket, and I'll leave here tomorrow. I didn't come over here to stay. I came over here to do a job."

So while we were sitting there—the Japanese had built us an officers' club—the prisoners, just a tent and all. They didn't need no building. They had a beautiful rock wall around the ocean there. We were sitting there with our feet up on the thing. One of the bartenders came over and said—I had made jaygee then—"Lieutenant Arbor, sir, you're wanted over behind the bamboo there." Well, that's where all the lieutenant commanders on up were. All the rest of us guys were over on this side of the curtain.

I said, "For what?"

About that time, I looked up, and here was a big commander saying, "You've been invited over on our side." I got up and went over there, and they wanted to know why I was born, all those same old questions. So one guy asked me, "How do you drink so much whiskey and never stumble? You're never incoherent and always polite."

I said, "Oh, I just drink as much as I want or can hold, and I never step over my bounds."

He said, "I see you don't."

So two or three weeks later, they had a boxing match up in the jungle. They had cleared off an area and had a boxing match between the Army and the Navy and the Marines there. The island had been secured then about three months.

Paul Stillwell: Admiral Nimitz was there at Guam then, wasn't he?*

Mr. Arbor: He hadn't come in. Before I left Pearl Harbor, I had begun to learn a little naval politics. So I was leaving the officers' club one night down at the submarine base, because everywhere I went, I had a jeep. Even when commanders and things couldn't get transportation, I always had a jeep everywhere I went.

Paul Stillwell: Why? How did you work that?

Mr. Arbor: I caught old big Dutch Schultz, who at that time was a tackle for the Chicago Bears, stealing my jeep to put on a submarine one night.† So I ran down to the dock. I said, "Say, fellow."

He said, "Go back. You can get transportation. I can't. You can't tell when you'll run into me again. Go on back up there. This ain't the only one we're going to get." I turned around and went back. As soon as I got back, "Don't go home. Go back in the officers' club and wait till it closes, and come out and look for your jeep."

So I thought, "I ain't got nothing to lose." I'd been doing this all along. I looked, and he had two or three jeeps. When I got to Guam, guess who was port director?

Paul Stillwell: Dutch Schultz.

Mr. Arbor: Dutch Schultz! He said, "Now look, Jess, I'm going to show you how you'll never get hurt in this war. I see your orders here say you can sign your orders to go anywhere you want in the Pacific, excepting back to Frisco. All you've got to do is put down 'inspectional duties.'" He said, "There ain't nothing on this rock for you to do. We'll have this R&R as soon as they get it out further advanced, and then go on to Saipan, Tinian, and Iwo Jima from here.‡ Now you attach yourself to the Seventh and Tenth Fleet on inspection. That's all one group of ships. Bull Halsey rides it so long, he

---

* In late January 1945 Fleet Admiral Chester W. Nimitz, USN, moved the Pacific Fleet headquarters from Pearl Harbor to Guam. He took with him only a relatively small staff, leaving the remainder of the staff in Hawaii.
† No player named Schultz appeared on Chicago Bears rosters of the early 1940s.
‡ R&R – rest and recreation.

pulls his flag down, and Nimitz steps aboard and raises his, so all them other little fellows can't get off. You can get off. You know that if you get on a ship close to Nimitz, you're not going to get hurt."*

I said, "Oh!" So that's what I did.

I came back to Guam, to get back to this boxing ring that night. I had my little jeep and went up in the jungle. I sat up there and was drinking that mountain dew, good whiskey. I looked around and saw the same little fellow that was always leaning over my shoulder, and I got to thinking, "What the hell?" He didn't have on any bars or anything. So I asked him if he was a news reporter.

He said, "No." But he never did tell me what he was. A few people around missed transportation out there in the jungle. He came over, stumbled over to me, and asked could he ride back to NOB with me.†

I said, "Yes."

He said, "Well, this is my last report on you."

I said, "What?"

He said, "I've been assigned to tail you from the moment you left Great Lakes." He showed me the report.

I said, "What was the report on?"

"To see how you conduct yourself, to see if there will be any more colored officers." You know, that was a hell of a burden to place on somebody like that.

Paul Stillwell: Whom did he work for, the Secret Service, the FBI?

Mr. Arbor: Secret Service. And I came to find out that Cooper and the rest of them, they all had one. Because they didn't make any more until '45. Then they started putting staff officers: chaplains, and doctors, and things like that in. They didn't have any more line officers.

---

* Admiral William F. Halsey, Jr., USN, served as Commander Third Fleet from 15 March 1943 to 22 November 1945. His counterpart, Admiral Raymond A. Spruance, USN, commanded the Fifth Fleet. So when the fleet command changed, Spruance, rather than Nimitz, took over. The same group of ships was known alternately as Fifth Fleet or Third Fleet, depending on which admiral was in command at the time.
† NOB – naval operating base.

Paul Stillwell: Well, men like Gravely were in that V-12 program.*

Mr. Arbor: Yes. They were in V-12.

Paul Stillwell: I think he was commissioned in '45.†

Mr. Arbor: Forty-five. That's when they started commissioning them out of the V-12 program. Then they started commissioning them. There was Lieutenant Commander Hope, who was working on his doctorate in engineering; he came in there as a lieutenant commander at the age of 37.‡ They sent him out to Pearl Harbor, and I ran into him. Thompson was the first doctor I saw, but he wasn't the first; he was almost the first.§ And Jones, right out of Harvard University School of Medicine, was the second one. The first chaplain was James Brown.** I saw him in July this year. He's retired out in Frisco now.

When I left the Pacific, we didn't know what the status was going to be after the war was over, so my CO on Guam wrote a letter to his brother, who, at that time, was in the Bureau of Naval Personnel. I've got the letter here now. He told me, "If you were married, I'd like to keep you with me here." Well, I hadn't thought about coming home, because I wasn't married. Hell, my mother was doing all right, brothers, sisters, everything getting along fine. He said, "Think it over."

The next day he called me and asked me if I'd given it any thought. I told him, "Yes, sir. If you think that much of my services, I'll come back." So he gave me 55 days to come home and get married. Well, I didn't any more know who I was going to marry any more than you did.

---

* Ensign Samuel L. Gravely Jr., USNR, was commissioned as a line officer in December 1944 through the V-12 program. In 1971 he became the Navy's first black admiral.
† Actually, Gravely was commissioned in December 1944.
‡ In May 1944 Dr. Edward S. Hope was commissioned as a lieutenant in the Civil Engineer Corps. He was then 42 years old. He was the first black officer in the Navy's CEC. He was promoted to lieutenant commander and was the highest-ranking black naval officer to serve in World War II.
§ Lieutenant (junior grade) Arthur Thompson, Medical Corps, USNR. Lieutenant (junior grade) Cyril Jones, MC, USNR. The first black Navy doctor was Lieutenant (junior grade) Bernard Robinson, MC, USNR. He was commissioned before the Golden 13, because the Navy mistakenly thought he was white.
** James Russell Brown, the Navy's first black chaplain, served on active duty from 26 April 1944 to 30 April 1946.

Paul Stillwell: Why did he want you to be married?

Mr. Arbor: Because they had built me a house out there on Guam. They were getting ready for peacetime buildup of the island, and he wanted me out there. I saw them building the house and everything. It was beautiful—landscaped and everything. I would have gone back, I'm telling you the truth, because I didn't have any trouble. I figured I could have gotten married if I had wanted to. But I caught that jungle rot. I couldn't go in swimming; I couldn't handle any citrus fruits. It would break out all on my hands, and occasionally breaks out on my foot now in the summertime. In the summertime, it breaks out, and if the weather gets like this, it will go away overnight. I've had everything from X-ray therapy down, and they tell me nothing.

So Barney Smith, that was his name, his brother was a captain in Washington and he was a captain out there. So I came here and got to running around, made a few connections, had a good job, everything like that. My feet had healed up, so I could walk out on my back porch. I was in the snow one night, went in the house, sat down, running my mouth. The next morning, I got up, and the thing was starting to heal up. So I stayed here about 30 days. I had to go out to Great Lakes, and they sent me down to Memphis to the naval air station down there on an errand for them. Now it was time for me to go to Washington. I came back home here and got me a grapefruit, sat down, and rubbed my feet real good, all up and down my arms, stayed up all night long just walking and running and drinking and going on.

I caught a plane, went out to the airport at the Navy base there. I got a flight out to Washington. I had written to his brother, so I walked into his brother's office. My hand was all swollen up, and my feet.

Paul Stillwell: From the grapefruit?

Mr. Arbor: Yes. He said, "What's the matter with your foot there, Lieutenant?"

I said, "Well, I caught that jungle rot out there in the Pacific, and it just takes time."

He said, "Oh, hell. George has been out on that damn island so long, he's rock happy. You go back out there, you're certain to lose a leg, boy." I broke down and started crying. He said, "Look at your hands there. Some people just can't stand the tropics, and you can't. I'm not going to send you back out there."

I said, "Will you write your brother and tell him?"

Before I left the island, he asked me if I was going regular Navy. I said, "The Navy has been experimenting with me and the rest of us. Now three years is three years. Four years for me—four years—and they don't know what they want me to do. If I knew the policies of the Navy, since I'm single, I might reconsider it."

So he said, "Why don't you sit down and write a letter to the Chief of the Bureau of Naval Personnel, bring it over here, and I'll help you word it." So I wrote the letter. He said, "This is good enough. I don't know why you spelled this word wrong. Give it to the yeoman." He typed a nice form letter and wanted to know the status of a Negro sailor, particularly officers, in the postwar program. So I got a nice reply to the effect that they would be considered on the basis as any other officer, for me to make a request if I wanted to transfer over. So I didn't. Nelson is the only one out of our group who did.[*]

Paul Stillwell: Why didn't you?

Mr. Arbor: I had gotten back here and got tied up with one of those old big-leg gals. After running around, I opened up my own business. You know, I've been one of those type of persons to adjust to any environment I'm in, see. I said, "Now I have served my country well. With the little salary rate they pay now, shoot, I can't stay in there for that." Now 20/20 hindsight is the best thing I've ever known. Had I known the potentials at that time—but knowledge only comes with age and experience—I would have stayed, because I think I could have done more in the Navy than I did out, because I would have been confined to the Navy, not here and there. It took me a long time before

---

[*] Of the Golden Thirteen, Dennis Nelson was the only one who made a career of the Navy. He retired as a lieutenant commander in 1979.

I could come down out of the clouds, see. If I had to do it all over again, I guess I only regret that I just didn't stay in longer.

Paul Stillwell: Nelson was really dedicated to the Navy, wasn't he?

Mr. Arbor: Yes, and egotistic! He was a character, but he was forthright, though. Nelson is the one who got all the rest of the officers put out of Great Lakes. Nelson had a 1940 convertible Mercury. He washed that car 365 days a year. If it was 20 below zero, he'd wash that car, and wouldn't let anybody else wash it. After Armstrong got busted out of Great Lakes, Commander Gumz came in and took his place, and his wife was coming from somewhere on the main side up there.[*] Nelson had that top back, with that cape flying in the wind on that February morning. He stopped and offered Commander Gumz's wife a ride. So they shipped Nelson right on out to Kwajalein. He turned right around and wrote them a nice letter, thanking them for sending him to that place, how nice it was. So I asked Nelson, "Nelson, when you applied for regular Navy, what was the extent of the conversation?"

He said, "Jess, they asked me . . ."—see, he didn't know anything about seamanship; he was strictly public relations. His major was history and somewhere in the soft sciences or social sciences. It wasn't in the hard sciences. He said they asked him, "What reason do you think that we should accept your application for the regular Navy, on what basis?"

He said, "I'm going to just reverse it. What reason would you deny my application?" So he mentioned that thing and transferred over. I have pictures of him where, wherever there was some publicity stunts going on or feats, he would always—and he wore his uniform beautifully, even when I've seen him with Queen Elizabeth on the *Queen Mary*.[†] How in the hell he got up on there, I don't know, but he's got pictures showing him. And did 20 years.

---

[*] Commander Donald G. Gumz, USN.
[†] Queen Elizabeth II has been Britain's monarch since 1952. *Queen Mary* was a British passenger liner.

The way I look at the Navy now, with the black officers who are in there, nobody is keeping any record on it. I make the National Naval Officers conventions, all of them.* I run into them, all those officers who have done 10, 12, some of them 18 years, and then get out, and they realize what's going on. Now, the way I see it, the Navy is programming those officers for defeat. They might pass out a recruiting bulletin of so and so, and so and so. All those officers—and most of them are coming out of the academy that I talk to. There's one up at Great Lakes right now. I told him the other day, "You're just a damn fool. When they pass over you for sitting around here clipping coupons and registration tickets and recruiting men, you won't have any sea duty." He'd been out to sea, I think, for 18 months. I said, "Now you're trying to get another half-stripe. As far as you'll get will be a full lieutenant. You've got to have so much sea duty, so many workshops, so many seminars, and so much schooling in the Navy's line. If they pass over you twice, you get your seabag and jump over the back fence, because, number one, you won't get a chance to reach that 20th year mark. It won't cost them anything. You stay in this man's Navy 14, 16, 18 years, and don't make it to 20, that's your fault."

When I was out there on the coast in July at the convention out there, I was talking to a bunch of those officers walking around there, full lieutenants, jaygees, one or two lieutenant commanders. I'd asked them those questions. One kid came up to my room and handed me a card and said, "I understand Secretary Lehman is coming over to see you all tomorrow."†

I said, "Yes. Is there any particular question you want me to ask him? I'm just stupid enough to ask anything, because John can't help me nor hurt me now."

He says, "Will you please ask him about those boards and commissions who rate officers for advancement once they pass full lieutenant?"

I said, "Now I don't know anything about that. I've only heard a few things about it, because it's been no concern of mine. I've been trying to find out why so many of you guys stay in the Navy 12, 14, or 16 years, and get out. My observation is that you are programmed for failure, regardless of how intelligent you are. Number one, you get to be

---

* The National Naval Officers Association is an organization of African American officers in the sea services – Navy, Marine Corps, and Coast Guard.
† John F. Lehman Jr. served as Secretary of the Navy from 5 February 1981 to 10 April 1987.

lieutenant commander or commander in a specialized field, and if you come out of Annapolis, you more likely will be in engineering or accounting. Here comes along one of these big companies, like Borg Warner or General Motors or U.S. Steel, who says, 'Commander, how much money—what is your salary?'

"'Why, I don't make but [I'll just use arbitrary figures] $80,000 a year.'

"'Is that all you're making? You come with me. I can start you off at $250,000 a year, with such and such perks.'" His eyes jump open. Guaranteed. Well, they can. Forget he's putting back 14 or 16 or 18 years, with all the perks for the rest of his life if he makes 20. He opts for this $250,000. He'll work 12 or 18 months, then some other conglomerate or merger or acquisition takes over this company and brings in his middle management, and out the back door you go. Then that's all you can do. You lost this over here in the Navy, and you can't stay here. You're too high priced, you're too educated to take the job that's open, so the next thing you know, you are groping around in the street. I see them all the time around these reserve officers' clubs—I make them, and I hear those stories.

So when I asked the Secretary about that, he looked at me and wanted to know where did I get that information. I told him. I said, "I can't use your name now."

"No," he said, "you can't use my name."

"That's all right. All I want you to do is give me the question. If I come to you for information, I just want you to give me the source."

He said, "The only source is the Secretary of the Navy or the board of commissions. So he can tell you."

When I asked him, he told it the exact way he told at our meeting: "I don't have any authority over those boards of commissions. That's a congressional appointment of civilians." He told me, "There's not one from the Middle West or the South; they're all from the East Coast or the West Coast." One thing he did say, he has the last word on those promotions, and sometimes he can hold them up, and he can recommend some. Naturally, he can't recommend too many admirals, because there's no room for them; so many captains, and no more commodores. So once you make captain, you've got your 30 years in, see.

But I told him, "Set your eyes for the stars, and you might hit a stump. But be sure you stay in these schools, every war college—the Naval War College, the Army War College, the Marine War College. They're paying you to go. You're not fighting."

"My wife doesn't want me to."

"Who in the hell did you marry? Is she in the service? Is she bringing the check home? Don't admirals all have wives and children? Don't get tied up in those skirts. If you can't bring them up, don't let them drag you down." That's the thrust of my work now. I try to tell them all, while they're in there, "Invest some of that money in something. Don't take it all and head for Las Vegas or on the East Coast in Atlantic City. Invest some of that money. Get a mutual fund, money market, something. Do the same with that money as you would if you were out in the street. That's because 20 years will pass in a hurry, and you'll be a darn sight better off when you come out, if you've got something to lean back on, whether you're physically incapacitated or as physical as a giant. Use your mentality."

I look at those fellows who went in with me. See, when we went in, there wasn't any such thing as a draft.* They were all volunteers. At the time I went in, you had to be a high school graduate to get in. That went on up until—I think it was '45, and the Secretary of the Army got mad and went to the House Armed Services Committee and told them, "Now look, since the general enlistment has been opened to colored in the Navy, the Navy is getting the cream of the crop, and they're sending all the dummies to us. Hell, we're fighting an unfair fight here."† That's when general conscription started, right there.

All those boys—practically everybody had one year of college or better when I went in. None of us hadn't finished high school. I had to represent the Navy for Black History Week aboard the *Carl Vinson* in February, and in scurrying around, to try to get a 15-minute speech, I went down to Washington.‡ Sam Barnes and myself went over to the

---

* On 16 September 1940 President Franklin D. Roosevelt signed the Selective Service and Training Act into law. It began the first peacetime military draft in U.S. history. In the early part of World War II it was still possible to volunteer for a specific service. From 1943 onward to the end of the war, all men entering the service were by conscription.
† During World War II the civilian head of the Army was the Secretary of War, a Cabinet position. In 1947 the civilian head became known as Secretary of the Army, a sub-cabinet billet.
‡ USS *Carl Vinson* (CVN-70) is a nuclear-powered aircraft carrier commissioned 13 March 1982.

Archives and over to the Library of Congress, looking back, stumbled upon so much stuff, that I didn't have time, so I just scribbled down a few things that I tried to use as a basis for the speech.*

I was surprised to find out that from 1776 down to 1914, that the stuff they were putting out on blacks in the Army and Navy was just skimmed over. Now I skimmed over this. From 1776 down to 1914, they didn't call them captains then in those days; they were ship's pilots. How many blacks? I just picked out a few of the heroes in there. They were in every branch of the service up until Woodrow Wilson got in there.† He's the one who, by executive order, said, "No, there can be a few in the black gang down in the boiler room, and all the rest will have to be mess attendants or stewards." And that stayed right there until 1 January 1941, when Franklin Roosevelt, under the urgings of his wife and Mrs. Mary McLeod Bethune, changed that order.‡ I've got to have this typed up; I scribbled this out. Now this is on record! It gives here the dates, times, places for reference. It's right in the Library of Congress. You know I didn't write it. I had intended to have this typed up, but I don't have a secretary. My wife's secretary is too busy now. This is nice reading here. I've got those files and things, cabinet full of things that I'm going to get assembled. Lieutenant Collins in Washington—he's out now after 18 years—says he's going to write a book. I told him he has access to the files out there. He says he has all the records he can dig up. His major was history, so he would have more interest than I, and the knowledge of where to find it.

I was talking to Ester Boone out on the coast last week.§ She said she didn't see why some of us haven't written. Nelson is the only one who compiled anything.** Have you talked to George Cooper yet?

---

* Dr. Samuel E. Barnes, a member of the Golden Thirteen, lived and worked in Washington, D.C., for many years.
† Woodrow Wilson was President of the United States from 1913 to 1921. In August 1919 the Navy stopped enlisting black men.
‡ Mary McLeod Bethune (1875-1955) was a black educator who in 1904 opened at Daytona Beach, Florida, a small school called Daytona Normal and Industrial Institute. It merged in 1923 with Cookman Institute to form Bethune-Cookman College, with Mrs. Bethune as president. It was on 7 April 1942 that the Navy, under prodding from President Roosevelt and his wife Eleanor announced that it would open general service enlisted ratings to blacks. The first to enlist under the new provision was William Baldwin, on 2 June 1942.
§ Ester Boone worked for many years in the Navy Recruiting Command on minority affairs.
** Nelson's master's thesis was published by the Navy Department in 1948 and later came out as a book, *The Integration of the Negro into the U.S. Navy* (New York: Farrar, Strauss and Young, 1951).

Paul Stillwell: No, I haven't yet.

Mr. Arbor: George Cooper has, if he didn't turn it all in to the museum there in Ohio, the black museum there, because we all, the year before last, turned in a lot of important stuff out of our files to that museum down there. He had a stack about this high.

Paul Stillwell: About two feet high.

Mr. Arbor: Now, whether he's still got it, I don't know, because George was the last—because Syl, Reginald Goodwin, he's dead, and George, and one other, they were Armstrong's boys.* So as long as he stayed there, he kept them in the battalions around Great Lakes. There wasn't but one camp open for blacks; that was Robert Smalls, so all the memos and directives that came from Washington came through Syl's office. When he left there, he went to Washington.

Paul Stillwell: You said Armstrong got taken out of there. What happened to him?

Mr. Arbor: I met him when he came to Pearl Harbor. He was walking down the road, and I picked him up in the jeep. He got so mad.

Paul Stillwell: Why?

Mr. Arbor: How can a little ensign be riding around in a 1940 light gray Plymouth? He couldn't get transportation from there out to the colored base. His father opened up Hampton Institute, so that made him an authority on everything black, even black shoes, old clothes. Anything black, he was an authority on it. That's on record. I was out to George Cooper's house about four years ago. He was showing me. He said, "Jess, I know you haven't seen all this crap, all this stuff that Armstrong stigmatized the Navy with because of his father's position."

---

* Reginald Ernest Goodwin was a member of the Golden Thirteen. He died before he could be interviewed by the Naval Institute's oral history program.

I said, "Well, George, you have to look at the source and the times. I'm not worried about what one individual says or what he does. All I want is history put in the proper perspective, because that's what I'm going to spend the rest of my life trying to do. I don't want anybody to stroke me. Just tell it like it is." I was just looking at the battles these boys went through and how it's recorded, just like it happened.

Paul Stillwell: What boys are you speaking of?

Mr. Arbor: The several I picked out of the book back to 1776, the battle that Perry had on Lake Erie, and on down through 1912, all like that.* Robert Smalls there, the one the camp is named for, who was a combination mess attendant and fireman.† That Saturday evening, when all the officers went ashore, he took the ship, with all the boys that didn't have liberty, just before dark, ran the blockade at Virginia, gave all the signals, signs, and turned the ship over to the federalists, a Union Army ship. That's why they named that camp for him. All that's recorded correctly, but you'll never hear anything about it. I was just listening to this controversy over Columbus yesterday. I said, "That's not the first thing, the first time. Even if he did come directly from Spain here, he couldn't "discover" America; he just came to America. There were people here when he got here. Same as if I come in your garage and "discover" your car and drive it out. I didn't discover the thing. I just found your car in your garage, where it's supposed to be." That's the reason I say history should be brought up correctly.

Another thing I tell—just like this city here. I see a street, a boulevard, a statue for every person who has accomplished anything in this city but the first settler here, du Sable, was black, *the* very first one.‡ They've got a little plaque right down here where he had his trading post, about the size of one of those certificates. You wouldn't know it

---

* Oliver Hazard Perry (1785-1819) was an officer in the fledgling U.S. Navy. He was famed for the victory of his force in the Battle of Lake Erie on 10 September 1813. He reported the result of the action with a brief message, "We have met the enemy, and they are ours."

† Camp Robert Smalls was the site of training for black recruits. It was named for an escaped slave who captured the Confederate steamer *Planter* during the Civil War and turned her over to the U.S. Navy. He served as pilot of the *Planter* and later of the gunboat *Keokuk*. After the war, Smalls (1839-1915) served in the U.S. Congress as a representative from South Carolina from 1875 to 1879 and from 1884 to 1887.

‡ Jean Baptiste Pointe du Sable was a Haitian colonist who was the first non-indigenous settler, around 1779, in what is now Chicago. In 1968 de Sable was declared the founder of Chicago by the state and city.

was there. But here was the soldier, Lee, Grant, every immigrant that came over here, who accomplished something—a big statue or a square somewhere. But the plaque is at the light there at Wacker and Michigan, right around the corner from that Hyatt Regency. If you didn't know where it was, if you weren't looking for it, you never would see it. Now they're trying to get the outer drive named for du Sable, but not one school named for him here. Wouldn't history be correct in erecting a statue for the first man to settle in Chicago?

Paul Stillwell: Sure.

Mr. Arbor: That's the thrust of my attempt just now, trying to get history in proper perspective.

Paul Stillwell: I'd like to get some more on your personal history. We started with the Navy experience. Could you go back to your boyhood and your parents and talk something about that?

Mr. Arbor: Oh, do I have to go through all that again? I'll start. I didn't know too much about my father's side, only his two older brothers and older sister. His mother died before I was born, but he had three brothers and two sisters. The land that was deeded to my grandmother on both sides after slavery—I remember my grandmother on my mother's side, because I was 35 years old when she passed at the age of 105.

Paul Stillwell: She had been a slave?

Mr. Arbor: She was 12 years old when slavery was abolished. My father went to school. As far as they would let him go in those years was fourth grade, and they started him teaching.

Paul Stillwell: Where was that?

Mr. Arbor: Arkansas. Now, the house that I think he was born in—I know his baby brother was born in it—still stands. They must have had four boys, because they would give you 20 acres and a mule for every boy. If you had ten girls, you didn't get anything; they gave it for the boys. Because they gave them a house and 80 acres of land. His mother died, he said, when he was about 14 years old, and his oldest sister had married, and his two oldest brothers had left home, so he just took his baby brother and baby sister. They worked the land, and they bought all the land around they could for $1.00 an acre, the whole wilderness then. So I think they ended up with around 200 acres of land. After my dad got married, his baby brother moved over to the next house with him and rented out part of the land. My father had ten boys and two girls on one side of the farm. His brother had ten girls and three boys on the other side. And the land is still there today.

On my mother's side, she must not have had but two boys, because she didn't get but 40 acres and two mules, and we still have that. Out of the ten boys and two girls in my family, three of them died before they were 21. All the rest of us who wanted to, finished college. There are six of us still living. Two are retired principals. One just refused to go into the school system, so he went into drafting; he's retired. My oldest sister, about 77, is a retired schoolteacher. My baby sister was teaching when she died. I wouldn't go in the classroom. I went into the engineering department, and I'm retired. So what I do now is go down and do volunteer work for the Navy.

Paul Stillwell: Where and when were you born?

Mr. Arbor: I was born in Arkansas, December 26, 1914.

Paul Stillwell: Whereabouts in Arkansas?

Mr. Arbor: A little place that only me and the good Lord knows, called Cotton Plant, Arkansas.

Paul Stillwell: How big a place was that?

Mr. Arbor: 1,661, up until the day I left, and there's never been that many since.

Paul Stillwell: How long did you live there?

Mr. Arbor: Until I was almost 16.

Paul Stillwell: Did the family then come to the Chicago area?

Mr. Arbor: Yes.

Paul Stillwell: What led to the move?

Mr. Arbor: Right after World War I, Mama's three brothers came up. One went to Buffalo, New York; two went to Flint, Michigan. So they came back there, I think, in 1924 or '25 and insisted on Mama and them leaving there. So we rented the place out and left. We stopped here and have been here ever since.

Paul Stillwell: What sort of work did your dad get into?

Mr. Arbor: Carpenter. All those men back in those days knew something and were carpenters, because you had to build your own house, see. He built his own wagons. We never had a toy for Christmas that he didn't make. We had a little old cap pistol or something like that, but a wagon and like that, he made them all. Chairs, brooms—all of that he made.

Paul Stillwell: Did you go to public schools in both Arkansas and here?

Mr. Arbor: None of us ever attended a public school a day in our lives, none of us.

Paul Stillwell: What schools did you go to?

Mr. Arbor: We went to Presbyterian Academy. Not one of us, either my dad's children or his brother's children, attended the public schools a day in our lives. I had to walk six miles a day round trip to get there.

Paul Stillwell: Was that in Arkansas?

Mr. Arbor: In Arkansas. Then when we came here, we went to Catholic schools.

Paul Stillwell: How would you compare the two school systems you were in, Arkansas and Illinois?

Mr. Arbor: Now, there is no comparison. The only difference I see, you had a library here. I never was in a library until the first day I went to college. Now you have libraries in all those schools. But the academic training and the discipline, you couldn't beat it. You didn't hear of anybody who couldn't read or didn't know how to spell or do math. At the school I went to, you had four years of Latin, one year of Greek, and Bible every morning as your first class. We had to take Bible, the New Testament, for English, and diagram an entire verse.

Paul Stillwell: Some of those sentences get pretty long.

Mr. Arbor: Whew! Eight parts of speech. By the time you got to the sixth or seventh grade, you knew all those. There was no such thing as a kindergarten school. When you went to school, you started school in the first grade. It got easier for me, because I had six ahead of me that helped me. My mother went to the eighth grade. Mama was ten years younger than my dad. Every year they would raise the level of those schools, because his last year in school was 1880-something. He was 69 when he passed. I have one uncle now in Flint, Michigan. He says he's 99, but he has to be more than that, because I'm almost 90 myself.* [Laughter]

---

* Mr. Arbor was 71 at the time of this interview.

Paul Stillwell: You're a young-looking 90, then.

Mr. Arbor: He was, I think, 21 or 22 when he went in the Army in 1918. You know he can't be 90-nothing! I asked him. He said the only thing he has is his old World War I Army discharge, and he won't let anybody see it. I understand he's in the hospital up in Flint now with arthritis, but he won't let nobody see that thing but the doctor. He won't turn it loose. He'll tell you, "You look and see and copy it off," and he'll put it up under his pillow. So I asked him, the last time I was there, "Uncle, why don't you want anybody to see your Army discharge?"

He said, "They've got my age messed up on it." But he is just as healthy. If he was sitting over here, you'd swear I am older than he. Just as agile, and didn't start deteriorating, as far as that arthritis is concerned, until last year. Has most of his teeth, he's not bald-headed, and not gray, and does not dye his hair.

Paul Stillwell: That's amazing.

Mr. Arbor: His mother was 105 when she passed, and she was never at a doctor but once in her life when she was seven years old. I asked her, "What did you go to the doctor for, Grandma?"

She said, "My master—I had the earache one Saturday, and he had to go to church that Sunday, so that Monday, he took me and my sister to see a doctor. The doctor asked him what was wrong with me. He said, 'She's got the earache.'

He said, 'Girl, what did you do to start your ear aching?'"

She said, "I just washed my hair."

He said, "Oh, go ahead home. Don't wash your hair no more." And she didn't wash her hair anymore from that day until she died.

Paul Stillwell: Gee!

Mr. Arbor: Just take some Blue Seal Vaseline. Her hair was down to her shoulders. She combed it with cotton—hair, the scalp just as clean. I don't know what she did when she was having all them 13 babies, how she took care of it. After she got old and everything, prepared her own food and combed her hair. That's all she did. All of her children lived to—my mother's oldest sister just passed at 106 last year or the year before that.

Paul Stillwell: It looks like you've got quite a few to look forward to.*

Mr. Arbor: That's what I say. I've got a long time before I make 100.

Paul Stillwell: Did you encounter prejudice when you were down in Arkansas? How was the situation there?

Mr. Arbor: I'll tell you what. We didn't encounter any, because all around us in that entire county, just about, there weren't that many white people around there. All blacks owned it, and did up until about ten years ago. Most of the kids were all grown and left there; they went back and sold it. We're the only ones in the neighborhood where we lived, still own it. One of them owns 20 acres. All the rest, those grandkids sold it. We just kept ours. We've always rented it out. Before my dad died in '39, after all his kids were grown and off, they rented it out to the government. All we did was pick up the check and pay the taxes up until about four years ago. Then they cut off crop support and thought we'd be forced to sell it to a big landowner. No. We didn't take anything. We pay the taxes, the rest of us who are living.

Paul Stillwell: Was Cotton Plant essentially an all-black town?

Mr. Arbor: Yes.

Paul Stillwell: What sort of municipal facilities, if any, did it have? Did it have stores, churches?

---

* Mr. Arbor lived until 11 January 2000, when he was 85.

Mr. Arbor: Yes, it had every denomination you could name. Two banks, a post office, three cotton gins, sawmill, factory where they made shirts for the Army, I guess about 20 or 30 stores. At one time they had three railroads running through it. It's always been a progressive town. High schools, two elementary schools, and I don't know whether the Baptist Academy was a high school or not. I left there before. But I know the Presbyterian school, because my older brothers and sisters and my Mama finished there. They went to high school. We've got a little old Cotton Plant club here now for offspring, and there's about 500 in that. We were just talking together the other day. I don't know anybody from there, not one, that's not either in a trade or profession. Nobody that I've ever seen from Cotton Plant went through that academy that you'd be ashamed to see in the street, because if they went there, you were forced to learn. You had to. You couldn't be late, no matter how far you lived from there, seven or eight miles, and you had to be there on time.

Paul Stillwell: So you learned discipline at an early age.

Mr. Arbor: And the old man was worse than that. My dad never did weigh no more than about 150 to 160 pounds, and every time one of his sons got 12 years old, he was larger than his dad. Mama weighed 200. The old man was soft-spoken, never used a word of profane language in his life. But, boy, was he rough on some boys. You couldn't play ball or shoot marbles on Sundays; he wouldn't whip you on Sundays, but if you had one coming, you got it before breakfast Monday morning.

Paul Stillwell: He saved them up.

Mr. Arbor: Saved them up. His first oldest boys he whipped every Monday morning the good Lord sent for the same thing: smoking. I was the youngest one in the bunch at that time, but I had it coming either way I went. My oldest brother would go to town that Saturday and get him a nickel sack of Bull Durham and put that in his pocket and let the tag hang out, and cover his shirt up, because he was 16 then. When we'd get up from the breakfast table Sunday morning, before we went to church, our table at home looked like a chow table with maybe 12 kids, and after Grandma and her grandson moved down there with us, we had 15 at the table every morning! My older brother was sitting on the end down there, and Papa was at the head, Mama and Grandma and the girls on this side. All the little boys around there looked like little pigs at a trough. My oldest brother would get through eating first, and he'd go right out of the house, under a big tree. He'd roll us all a cigarette and give it to us. If we didn't smoke it, he was going to whip us.

Paul Stillwell: So you were between a rock and a hard place.

Mr. Arbor: If we did smoke it, my papa would come out there, "One, two, three, four, five. One, two, three, four." He'd say, "Now, you should know better," pointing at me. Why didn't he tell the old buzzard in front there at breakfast that it was coming?

After we all got grown, we used to go catch him and hold him and whip him. I'd say, "Now, we're giving you this whipping for the times we got caught. Why didn't you take us up in the woods or somewhere, a different place?" I don't know how long we did it; I know it was over a year.

All of us had to go to church every Sunday. He'd sit on one side, make us all line down, and he was sitting on the corner. Mama would sit over on the next corner with the baby, always had a baby, and watching. You'd better not go to sleep or punch anybody. Just like this, all day long. But not one of us has ever been in trouble of any kind, unless someone got caught in a poker game. But all of us went to school, and all of us who have children, which is not many, we always swore there wouldn't ever be that many of us sitting around the breakfast table if ever I get grown. Out of ten boys and two girls, there are seven grandchildren, and I have three of them.

Paul Stillwell: You've got more than your share.

Mr. Arbor: I've got more than my share. But all of them had to go to school and did. My three are all out of college and working.

Paul Stillwell: When you came up here to Illinois, did all of your family come, or did some stay back in Arkansas?

Mr. Arbor: No, some stayed in Arkansas for two or three years, something like that. But we always did work together as a family. Very, very few of the boys ever got grown at home anyway, because his theory was, "One man to a house, and—"

Paul Stillwell: He'd be the man.

Mr. Arbor: "I'm the man. When you think you know as much as I know, or can do better for yourself than I can do for you, there's the door." But he said, "Now, if you leave here and hit it hard, don't come back until you're 21." And he meant that. The first four oldest boys, the first two—my oldest brother, the one that left, he left at only 17, and had finished high school and had been in college two years, and decided he wanted to come home because his baby brother and his baby sister hadn't started school, so he just wanted to see them.

Paul Stillwell: Just for a visit?

Mr. Arbor: Yes. He came home in January. He wouldn't have been 21 until March 16. He came around on a bike in the snow that night. We let him in. He got up in the bed in the middle of us; we were going to warm him up. My dad came in there with that razor strap, whipped him. He jumped out the window, took the window sash and all. He told him, "You won't be 21 until March. Come back in March."

Paul Stillwell: Gee.

Mr. Arbor: And my next oldest brother would have been 21 in July. After college was out, he thought he'd come home and visit Mama. They said, "You won't be 21 until August." And, you know, Mama never said a word. I left when I wasn't quite 16. I came back home one day before I was 21, but he got my birthday mixed up. He thought I was born Christmas Day, but I was born the day after Christmas. He didn't realize it until the next morning. They were all singing "Happy Birthday." He had a big Adam's apple underneath. He said, "Boy, you're still lying, aren't you?"

So I started for the door, because I said, "I can't fight the old man." I came home and had my big college sweater on. He had been reading about me in the *Chicago Defender*, how I'd been playing football and all like that.*

He said, "You're a man this morning, but you were a liar yesterday.' He was a man of his word. I never got one penny. My daddy hadn't given me a solid quarter one time in his life. He'd give us all a dime or 15 cents on Sundays; you had to put a nickel of that in church. He said, "You can save a nickel of that if you want, or you can spend it all and get no more until Sunday." I'll never forget that.

At night, everybody had to sit down around that fireplace and get a book and read out loud, take turns reading. We didn't know for a long time that Papa couldn't read seventh and eighth grade work. We didn't know it, and Mama didn't tell us. Mama could. He'd make you go over it. He said, "Go back over it." If you stumbled over a word, he didn't know whether it was right or wrong, but you didn't say it smooth enough, so you had to go over it again. He'd say, "Go over that again, boy. When you get through, take your brother over here now." That's how it came on down.

He made all the boys sleep upstairs. Before you went upstairs to go to bed, you'd kneel at the foot of his bed and say your prayers. He kept what he used to call a little old mason jar, like this, full of change all the time. He had two $20.00 gold pieces and one or two $10.00 ones. My older brother taught us how to borrow a little from the old man. He said, "Those thick ones, you don't touch those, because he'll miss those, see. He won't miss that other change." So when you prayed, you just—

Paul Stillwell: Did you put your hand in the jar when you were praying?

Mr. Arbor: No, in his pocket. He'd be in the bed asleep. We didn't know he was asleep, because he could go to sleep in a minute, but if he pulled up, you'd put that back. A penny or a nickel or dime, a penny was something in those days. Whatever you got, you

---

* The *Chicago Defender* was a black newspaper with national circulation.

had to bring it to the older brother, all to him, and then he'd divide it and give you a nickel or a dime, and he'd keep the rest.

The last time I touched the old man up, that night when I got ready to leave home on my 21st birthday, to show him I was still a good Christian, after he got in the bed, he was talking and telling everybody his son came. He had saved a few of the clippings and things out of the paper from two or three years earlier. So I kneeled down on the floor at the foot of the bed. I think I was praying out loud that night so he could be sure. I looked and he was sleeping. I eased out $8.00, and I didn't go back anymore until he was real sick. But I sent that $8.00 back, see, from the payday I made. At the Chicago Beach Hotel, I made eight and a half dollars a week. I sent him $8.00, and the next week I sent him $8.00, and every week thereafter, I sent him at least $1.00. They weren't paying off in checks in those days; they just put it in an envelope and gave it to us. There weren't any off days—seven days a week.

Paul Stillwell: Where were you working then?

Mr. Arbor: Chicago Beach Hotel, 51st and Lake.

Paul Stillwell: When did you start there?

Mr. Arbor: Nineteen thirty-four, after the world's fair—1935.[*]

Paul Stillwell: So that was just after you turned 21.

Mr. Arbor: Yes.

Paul Stillwell: What work did you do there?

Mr. Arbor: I was doorman and receiving clerk. I worked there until '36, when Social Security cards came out—'37. Teachers were making then about $90.00 or $100.00 a

---

[*] The Century of Progress International Exhibition was staged in 1933-34 to celebrate the city's centennial.

month or something like that. I was making more than that out at the hotel, because they raised me up to $60.00 a month plus tips, and those lawyers and things coming out of school, all those other teachers, they went to the post office. They were paying $70.00 or $80.00 a month. So I didn't want that. I said, "I don't want no prestigious job that ain't paying anything." What I was getting was food and tips. I was making twice as much as they were, and I stayed there on the door until 1939. The vice president of the Pullman Company came through there one day and said, "Say, weren't you in the school yearbook?"[*]

I said, "Yes."

He asked me about—I forget his son's name.

I said, "Yes, we were classmates."

He said, "What are you doing standing up on this door? With the education you have, why don't you do something commensurate with your education?"

I said, "Mr. McMannen, I need not tell you why I'm on this door. The jobs that I can get commensurate with my education do not pay as much as this."

He said, "Well, why don't you go out here and get on the railroad then?"

I said, "They are not hiring anybody. They posted a list three weeks ago that they would not hire any more in five years."

So he reached in and said, "Take this card. Go down to 18th and L, and tell George Bulow I sent you."

I said, "Yes, sir.' I just put the card in my pocket. He had a '37 La Salle, and I got the car and brought it to the door, and he got in and left town. At that time, he was connected with the Washington Park racetrack. He left then, went down to Florida somewhere and came back about two weeks later, and I was standing up on the door.

He said, "Didn't I tell you to get off this door?"

I said, "Yes, sir."

He said, "Why didn't you do it? Where's that card?"

I told him I didn't know where it was.

He gave me another one and said, "You go down there." He got on the phone right at the door there and called down there and told them that I would be down there,

---

[*] The Pullman Company, based in Chicago, manufactured sleeping cars for railroads.

and put me on. So I told him, "Mr. McMannen, I appreciate your every effort, but you know I hate to get out there on that railroad, which runs according to seniority. I'll make one trip from here to California or New York or somewhere, come back, and some old-timer will bump me."

"You can't be bumped."

I said, "Then, too, the difference between the salary out there and here, it doesn't warrant my changing."

He said, "I'll tell you what. If you don't go, you can't work here."

Now I was between a rock and a hard place. So I went on down that evening. When I got there, they were looking for me and sent me out that day, and I didn't know anything. I stayed out there for two years. He left town, and then I came on back.

I said, "I didn't go to school or learn a trade to work for somebody else." I had learned how to make clothes then, see. I could draft and make. So I went downtown to Hart Schaffner & Marx. "No, no." I saw a friend of mine who said, "I can get you on over at Kuppenheimer's, but you can't be no draftsman."

I said, "If you can get me through the door, I can get to be a draftsman." So they took me as a porter. That was night work now, see, because almost all draftsmen and tailors were European. They were working overtime. They weren't making any money either, but they were working. So I kept watching them and watching them.

One time I went over. A guy got kind of halfway sick there. He had so much he had to get out every evening before he left. So I told him, "How are you going to do this? You're having cramps. You're old."

He said, "I've got to do it to get a job out, to get my family some food. I got no way else to work."

I said, "Mind if I give you a little hand?"

He said, "You won't be able to do this, boy." I grabbed that thing and sat down, and he looked at me. I couldn't make coats. In those days—see, there's nothing to a coat on the outside; all the guts are inside. All that was done by hand. I could do that pretty good, and that was his specialty, cutting pants, sleeves, pockets, all like that. I'd cut them out and make a pair of pants in about an hour. He saw that I could do that, and he kept on playing sick until he taught me all that.

Then they came in and caught me doing it one day. "Why didn't you tell us?"

I said, "You never gave me a chance to tell you."

"Can you read blueprints?"

I said, "I can draw them."

So they set up a partition and put me over behind it. I worked there and never made so much money in my life. Some weeks I'd make $150.00. I didn't know there was that much money in the world! Working, making tips, I'd done that on Christmas, holidays, but regular salary? I didn't know anybody had a salary like that. In 1940, I opened up my own shop. I had ten people working for me. Of course, I was fast then, so when I came out of the service, I went back in my business. You couldn't buy material then. Everything was short. You couldn't get any help, couldn't get any equipment. Because I just gave it all away when I went in. Then by the time I got reopened, this urban renewal came through, and they tore down everything just about from 39th Street out to 61st Street, before they put that [unclear] line through there, and all the way over to the lake. And my business went to pot.

That's when I went back to the board of education. I had gotten married then and had three kids, and one was finishing high school. I had to get something steady to be sure that they could go to college. My wife was teaching. I said, "I don't want to teach." I got in the engineering department. I was lucky how I got that. I didn't go down there to get in the engineering department. I went down there to see what was on the civil service board that I wanted to do.

When I went down to city hall and up to the civil service commissioner's office, somebody said, "Hi, Arbor!"

I said, "Hello."

"Where are you going now?"

I said, "I'm going on upstairs." I didn't know who I was talking to.

He said, "You don't remember me?"

I said, "No."

He said, "You know Reggie Goodwin?"

I said, "Yes, we were commissioned together."

He said, "Remember Reggie had a car?"

I said, "Yeah, he had a 1940 convertible Packard."

He said, "Sure. You remember when you all got your commissions, you all came down to Northwestern Station to pick up his brother?"

I said, "Uh-huh." He was 16 then. I said, "Yes. Where's Reggie?" So we were talking. I didn't know he went on back to finish law. He was over at the Criminal Court Building. I said, "I'll drop by to see him. I haven't seen him."

He said, "Where are you going?" That's after he told me who he was. He said, "I'm Reggie's brother. I'm the little brother you all came down to pick up in the snow in that Packard."

I said, "Oh, yes!" So I walked along with him, and he went on through this door, talking. I went on in with him. I walked in and sat down. He went over behind and sat at a desk. I didn't know what he was doing.

So I told him my plight. He said, "Go down there on the board and see what you can do and come back."

I went down there and looked. They had certified public accountants, all that stuff like that. I said, "I don't see anything I would want to do."

He said, "What can you do?"

I said, "Run my mouth and boss like hell." That's exactly what I told him.

So he said, "In your business, didn't you have steam boilers?"

"Oh, yes. Lightweight boilers."

He said, "The difference between lightweight and heavyweight boilers is the pressure applied."

I said, "I know that."

He said, "Why don't you go over to the board of education?"

I said, "No, there's too many [unclear] in the school system now."

"Why don't you try the engineering department?"

I said, "I don't know anything about those big boilers."

"You know the little ones. You can apply that knowledge to the big ones. Go over there and take this card. [I forget that woman's name.] Tell her I sent you."

So I went over there and asked for her. I didn't say I could back up my words, because if they put me in a high school where they had all that equipment, I couldn't handle it. If I get in an elementary school, I could handle it, because I had been in it.

So I went back over there. I said, "I want to speak to Mrs. Vannais Brook."

"What do you want?"

I said, "I want to speak to Mr.—"

"She's out." I saw a woman sitting over at a desk.

So I went on back and said to Reggie's brother, "Mrs. Vannais Brook is out."

He said, "No, she's not. She went in there before when we were coming in here. You go over there and tell them I'm the one that gave you the card."

The lady looked up and saw me. I said, "I came to see Mrs. Vannais Brook. This man sent me." She looked up. I didn't know I was talking to the civil service commissioner! He had made civil service commissioner of Chicago at that time.

Paul Stillwell: Goodwin's brother.

Mr. Arbor: Yes. She looked at that card; she got on the phone and called him. So I told her just what I told him, "I ain't looking for a job." I came out, and before I got back in this house, the phone was ringing. When I walked in, the phone was ringing. They sent me to a school the next day.

Paul Stillwell: What year was that?

Mr. Arbor: Nineteen sixty-eight. And I stayed there until they closed in '84. They found out I was 70 years old, and they kicked me out. But I started to school the next week, at night, boning up on it. I applied a little common sense with practical experience with the theory. All we had to do was keep a file on the desk, and if something big broke down, you'd call the district office anyway. But an ordinary thing, like watching the pressure or if something small would break down, I knew how to fix that. I wasn't looking for it to blow up. I could apply that and look in the book, change a valve. If it burns out, you're going to have a new one put in anyway. If you can't handle something, you call your supervisor. But I had sense enough to fix it in that office so they wouldn't put me in a high school, but an elementary school, a small building, only two boilers. If one would break down, you'd light up the other one, and call somebody in to fix it. That's all the rest of them were doing. And make out the payroll for the janitor, the paperwork, and see that the work was being done. I told them I could boss like hell. I stayed right there until a few years ago, at age 70.

Paul Stillwell: You told me that you didn't finish college in Arkansas because of your eligibility. Did you give any thought after that to getting your degree?

Mr. Arbor: No. Now, Baugh went back. Baugh went back to Arkansas; he left there six months before he got his. He went back, and then he went on to MIT and got his master's in engineering.[*] But I was making so much money, I said, "What's the use going back for three months?" I took some extension courses, and I've been in various night courses and things, but nothing leading to those three months just to say I have a degree.

Paul Stillwell: You talked about the Pullman man giving you his card and saying you should have a job commensurate with your education. Why is riding a Pullman any more commensurate than standing on a door?

Mr. Arbor: Paid more money and met a diversified class of people. See, there weren't airplanes in those days. I'd run into Helen Hayes and Presidents.[†] Everybody rode Pullmans.

Paul Stillwell: What railroad were you on?

Mr. Arbor: I was in a Pullman, all of them. By him sending me over, I could go anywhere I wanted to go. The second time I left Chicago, I stayed out 55 days before I

---

[*] MIT – Massachusetts Institute of Technology, Cambridge, Massachusetts.
[†] Helen Hayes was a famous stage actress.

came back. I told them, "Let me run wild." I'd go from here to, say, Los Angeles. Instead of going on to Florida or back to Seattle from Los Angeles, and I'd call down to San Diego and see what they had, or Oakland or Frisco. If I went to New Orleans, wherever I went, I wouldn't come back here. See, I wasn't married. I'd go to New Orleans, and if I didn't have a round trip, I'd go to Orlando or Miami. Of course, went to Boston. You knew you were coming back through New York if you didn't have a round trip. But if you came to Chicago, you got to get down. Nothing goes through Chicago; everything—I don't care what direction—stops here. I knew that. So if I could stay out of Chicago, I could stay on the road, and I just loved going around to these different museums and parks, things like that I had read about in school.

Paul Stillwell: That's the kind of job I heard, though, that there wasn't much sleeping at night.

Mr. Arbor: Four hours. Four hours a night. But, see, you're working, used to be, three days and three nights from here to Los Angeles, but they'd always have two Pullman cars together. Tonight you'd go to bed early, I'd hook into your car. Tomorrow night, I go to bed early, and you'd take the late watch in my car. So if the bell rang in my car, it rang in yours to show what section to go to.

Paul Stillwell: So you'd just switch off.

Mr. Arbor: Yes. When you saw a Pullman, you saw two or four, unless it was a little old overnight run like from here to Detroit or St. Louis. You start late, so people go to bed, and they didn't need you. You'd go to bed when the folks went to bed.

Paul Stillwell: But you decided after a while that wasn't for you?

Mr. Arbor: That wasn't for me. No job was for me; I don't care what it paid. I just always wanted to be in business for myself. That's what I tried to teach my kids, but you can only give them the tools to work with and let them select what they want to do.

Paul Stillwell: You had come from this all-black environment, being in Arkansas. Were there any adjustments to make coming into the integrated environment in Chicago?

Mr. Arbor: I've never had any trouble adjusting any place, ever, even when I went overseas. Those natives, every place I went, it wouldn't take me long to understand enough of the language and customs to blend. I might not could write it or read it, but if I talked with you long enough, I'd pick up on the essentials, like "food, water, bread, yes, no, come, go." Everywhere I went, they could understand "Coca-Cola" and [unclear]. So you learn the basic things first. I don't care where I go. If you give me three or four days of constant one on one, you point to this and tell me what it is, I know I won't say it correctly, but I'll get the basis of it. In the same vein, when you talk to them, they want to learn English. You point to this and you tell them, "Paper, bread, water, food, shoes, mouth, hair, eyes, head." That's the way I learned it.

I used to go down to Mexico when I was on the road. Every time I'd hit San Diego, I'd head across the border, just so I could try to learn conversational Spanish. Having had four years of Latin in school, one in Greek, I felt that Latin was the toughest thing, because you couldn't apply that to anything but medicine. All your words had Latin derivatives, but unless you got in the medical field like that, you didn't talk any Latin, but I had to take it.

Paul Stillwell: It helped you understand English better, really.

Mr. Arbor: Oh, yes. But in the English language and grammar they're using now, you'd have been better off not having suffered through all that stuff 50 years ago!

Paul Stillwell: Were you a good student?

Mr. Arbor: Fair. Fair. I was a good C or B-minus in everything but math, trig, and geometry. I passed, that's all. In the social sciences, where you could theorize and like that, I made A-minus or something like that—sociology, psychology, and that kind of stuff. One man's theory is no better than the other's; only the results are going to matter.

Paul Stillwell: Were you aiming toward a specific major at Arkansas State?

Mr. Arbor: I started out and had scholarships to go in the ministry, to tell the truth. So when I went there, I went into biology, but that stuff was almost like taking medicine. If I could have been better in the hard sciences, like chemistry or physics, the practical work in biology was interesting to me. But I really didn't know how to study, to tell the truth. The school didn't have any chemistry laboratory. I think I had seen one Bunsen burner. Had I ever? I knew H_2O equals water and NaCl, H_2SO_4, sulfuric—I learned that in third or fourth grade. But I'd never had the hands-on experience of applying it and doing an experiment until I got in college.

I'll never forget the first time I was in a library. I looked around like I was lost. I had to take six months of library science before I could check a book out at night. The other boys came out of those high schools and things with libraries, but I'd never seen one. I could spell it, spell anything I heard pronounced correctly. I could spell it. That was my handicap, but I knew that. There was one boy there who was good in math, and I was pretty good in history. So when we'd go to the dormitory at night, when dinner was over and football practice, I'd head down to Donald's room and make him teach me math. Then he couldn't remember his name when it came to history or the social sciences or psychology. I'd take him up to my room. If I was in his room, I couldn't teach him anything about that. And the same setting if he came to my room.

For math, I had to go to his room to learn. I guess that's from going to school too long. You have certain things in the recesses of your mind; you just can't get rid of them. I'd take him down to my room, if I didn't feel like reading, on the way from football practice or somewhere. And one old boy there was a genius. This Evelyn Wood reading, I think he had that when he was born. He could scan through a book and come up with a perfect A on anything in history or social science that he read. I'd read just enough to get in a conversation with him and say something wrong; he would correct me. I have a retentive memory. I'd lay right there and get me a B.

I'll never forget my first exam in trig. They'd seat you alphabetically. I forget what this old girl's name was. She was so homely, wouldn't anybody dance with her. Her last name had to be a B, because she sat right to my right. So we had a class of 31, our first exam. I had a little old English professor there. He came in, "We're going to have a little mental gymnastics this morning. Everybody put aside your books and break out your pencils and pads." Up on the board he wrote a problem. There wasn't but one number in it—something like sine over cosine, or cosequel something equals four, I don't know. He said, "I'm going down the hall a few minutes. Don't you all disturb each other." Well, he came back, and it was time to call for the papers. There was one A, one B, one C, and all the rest of them flunked. I made the B. I sat there and looked. That girl had a paper this long. I copied everything but her last name. If he hadn't come in there, I was going to copy that, because I thought that was part of the problem. He knew it was wrong, if I passed. So he said, "Well, it must be something I did to have this many flunked. We're going to give it over." He knew I hadn't passed it, so he gave it over again. He stayed in the room. I copied off a D on the next one. She was so fast and good with it. So from then on, I started dancing with her at those football dances, so she'd hold her paper so I could see.

Paul Stillwell: Hoping some of that would rub off.

Mr. Arbor: Then after they found out what I was doing, all those old football players tried it. They said, "Nuh-uh." She couldn't dance. I would sure like to know where that girl is. She helped me through. All I can remember in that trig classroom for the whole entire year, one axiom, when two variables are so related so that when the value of one is given, the value of the second can be determined also, and vice versa. Now I don't know what it means, but I remember that axiom. I never did find out what a variable was.

Paul Stillwell: How good a football player were you?

Mr. Arbor: Oh, I did all right.

Paul Stillwell: What position did you play?

Mr. Arbor: Right tackle. I did pretty well. That's the only way I got through.

Paul Stillwell: You must have been good to have all those scholarship offers.

Mr. Arbor: One of the greatest mistakes I think I made, I could have made the Chicago Cardinals before it was the St. Louis Cardinals, but they offered me only $500.00.[*]

Paul Stillwell: What year was that?

Mr. Arbor: Nineteen thirty-nine, because I had gone to the roads then. They were going to give it to me all at once, and that was contingent that I made the team. I had never heard but two black boys making professional football at that time, Duke Slater and Marion Motley.[†] They were so darn good, I didn't figure I was that good, and they were in the backfield. No lineman ever gets much credit for anything. So I thought, "If I go out here and lose this job and don't make the team and don't get that $500.00, I am in bad shape."

Paul Stillwell: Who was the coach then that was after you? Conzelman?

Mr. Arbor: No.

Paul Stillwell: Bidwill owned the team.[‡]

Mr. Arbor: Bidwill owned the team, but the coach is who I'm trying to think of.[§] Halas was with the Bears, nobody but him, so you can't forget him.[**] I can't think of who the coach is now.

---

[*] The Chicago Cardinals were in the National Football League for many years before moving to St. Louis prior to the 1960 season. In 1988 the team moved to Phoenix and became the Arizona Cardinals.
[†] Fred W. "Duke" Slater played in the National Football League from 1922 to 1931. In two of his seasons, 1927 and 1929, he was the only black player in the NFL. Marion Motley started his professional career with the Cleveland Browns of the All-America Football Conference in 1946. There were no black players between 1931 and 1946.
[‡] Charles Bidwill owned the team from 1933 until his death in 1947.
[§] Ernie Nevers coached the team in 1939 and Jimmy Conzelman from 1940 to 1942.
[**] George Halas was the long-time coach and owner of the Chicago Bears.

Paul Stillwell: Did you have a tryout?

Mr. Arbor: Yes. Certain prospects were good, but in those days, if you had a job, you married it. It was just one of those things. I got this. I might be like the dog with the bone in his mouth, barking, walking across a log. I might fall off the log, but I know I have this. I just had gotten down in there and had two or three kids over here at the International House and Chicago University. I was running in there, and I bought me a new car and three or four of those $14.98 suits with two pair of pants, and I was doing all right. I was able to give my mother some money every weekend. My dad was sick, and I'd give him some money. So I couldn't afford to.

Paul Stillwell: Right. When you went into the Navy, you sure had to take a cut in pay.

Mr. Arbor: Sure did. Sure did, but I was the last single man in draft board seven.

Paul Stillwell: You didn't have much bargaining power.

Mr. Arbor: I didn't have any! The guy that had been looking out for me, they drafted him. His draft board was at 51st and Lake Park, and mine was 47th and South Park. I think they met every Monday night then, whatever night they met, well, my name being Arbor, he'd pull my card out. No computer or nothing like that. So one day I came in town. Every time I'd come in town, I'd call him. One day when I called him, he said, "Your papers are in the works. I've been over there looking out for you, and they've drafted me!" That's why I took off to Mexico. He said, "Everyone's got to go, Jess. When they found your name in there, and they wanted to know how the heck I had gotten by." I wasn't 4F or 1F or 2B or anything.* "How did they overlook me? I couldn't tell them a lie."

We thought the war was going to be over in 30 or 60 days, because I remember I met a naval officer and his mother on the train. That's the first time I ever heard of Pearl

---

* The classification of 4F meant someone was ineligible for the draft for medical or mental reasons.

Harbor; I thought that was my baby sister's name. She was just on his arm, just crying in the dining car, "Oh, we're in the war!"

He said, "Ah, Mother, that won't last over 90 days. We're going to wipe them out." He was walking up, and looked good in his little Navy uniform.

I thought, "What is he talking about, Pearl Harbor? Who is she?" I knew a gal named Pearl Booth, but I didn't know Pearl Harbor. And in a year's time, I was in Pearl Harbor.*

Paul Stillwell: When did you go to boot camp?

Mr. Arbor: September the 11th, I reported to Great Lakes, 1942, left there after service school in December of '42. I spent Christmas in Boston.

Paul Stillwell: So you were about two months in boot camp.

Mr. Arbor: I think it was 12 or 14 weeks; I've forgotten.

Paul Stillwell: That long. What are your recollections of that training? Did that take some adjustment after this high life you'd been leading?

Mr. Arbor: That was the worst part of it. See, I'd been wearing those Thom McAn shoes. I'd never had a pair of Stetsons on. They cut my hair pretty high, heels, and they were wearing them too small, had bad feet, had blisters on my feet. I was trying to look pretty. When they put those thick-soled shoes on me and walked me from main side back over, my feet had swollen. I sat down and pulled out my little old pocketknife and cut those shoes up. I was standing up there in line the next morning at muster. A little chief about this tall said, "What's the matter with your shoes there, Mac?"

I said, "Sir, they hurt my feet."

He said, "You're in the Navy now, boy. Didn't anybody send for you; you volunteered. When you're in the Navy, you do what you're told, when you are told, and

---

* Arbor first got to Pearl Harbor in 1944, after he'd been commissioned as one of the Golden Thirteen.

how you're told." He walked up and hit me in the chest. "Now," he said, "get out of that line." He took me out and walked me all the way back over to main side, got me another pair, and threw them and hit me in the chest, "Now put those on." He walked me all the way back over there.

Paul Stillwell: Did they fit as bad as the first pair?

Mr. Arbor: They did give me my size. I had on 11s. I was supposed to have 12Ds. I got back over there and sat down and just cried. I missed chow. I sat down and just cried. I rubbed my feet, took a hot shower. We didn't have any bunks. I got up in that hammock and sat up all night long. First thing next morning, I could put the shoe on. I don't know if I was frightened or mad or what, but I knew I couldn't afford to mess up. I knew that. I wore my feet down. I haven't had a corn or a blister or bunion or blistered heel since, because I learned to get my size. That same little old chief didn't like me, because I had never pulled KP or guard duty the entire time I was in boot camp or in service school.[*]

After I got there, all of us were raw rookies, but one little old boy from Kansas City, he was 18 years old and just had finished high school, and he had had ROTC training.[†] But I hadn't had any. I don't think anybody in the group had any but Duck. So they put me in charge of the company, apprentice company commander, to learn how to drill. Duck was so small, they put him up there for the right guide. So they were teaching us how to drill—left, right, left, right—so Duck got out of his bunk one night and came and hit that hammock. "Shh, dummy. Don't say anything. Come on, come on." We got up and went in the head, and he taught me how to call cadence. He said, "Don't be so darn dumb. I'm going to make a man out of you. But you're going to have to keep those boys from whipping me tomorrow."

I said, "Okay, Duck, if you teach me how to drill." Every night in the head, we'd go down for two or three nights. Left, right, left, right. "How do you do stop them from forward march?"

---

[*] KP – kitchen police, known in the Navy as mess cooking.
[†] ROTC – reserve officers' training corps.

"Dummy, don't you know how to give a command to keep them from walking into the wall?" That's just how he taught me.

Paul Stillwell: Why was he afraid that something was going to happen to him?

Mr. Arbor: He was the smallest thing. You know how it is with raw recruits. You're going to pull pranks on them. Big boys whip them, you know, initiate them.

Paul Stillwell: So he was looking to you to be his protector.

Mr. Arbor: I was his daddy. We went all the way through boot camp like that. They put another old boy in charge, and he was supposed to have had ROTC. Came to find out, he hadn't. So they put me in charge, and I picked up so quickly, I wouldn't walk but that far from Duck. "Left, right, left, right. To the rear, march. Right face." He taught me all of it.

Paul Stillwell: Where did he know it from?

Mr. Arbor: He had had four years of ROTC in high school. When we got out of boot camp, he went to signalman's school, and I went to quartermaster's school. We were right across from each other and shared the same deck out there. They made me master-at-arms, so you know when I put up a watch list, I wasn't going to put my name on it! So I kept Duck's name off. I never did let him stand duty, KP or watch duty in the barracks, because of the way he had treated me.

When I'd come into the city, I'd bring him in with me, take him by the house. He'd sit down. Mama would look at him and say, "Jess, do they take little babies like this in the Navy?" He'd feel so embarrassed and all like that.

The best deal we ever had—let me tell you about the worst. They gave me five men to take to Boston when we left school, and went to the receiving barracks up there. They called us, "Men, lash up your seabags in seagoing fashion. These men report in: Arbor, Jess. Brusart, C., Brown, Applewhite. And didn't call Duck Collins and [unclear] That would have been the entire group that went from there.

So Duck said, "Arbor, Arbor, they didn't call my name. I want to go with you." So he ran downstairs and said, "You missed one name."

He said, "What name? No, you're going to Portsmouth, New Hampshire."

He fell down on the floor, just started crying, "I want to go with Arbor."

So I didn't see Duck anymore until the week we got our commissions. He was coming back through, going to Kansas City, and he didn't know that I was down there in school. He hadn't heard anything about any black officers. So I came by the house, and Duck was there. He saw me in my uniform and the second I had that on, he just stood and cried. He opened up the coat and said, "Son, I'm proud of you. How did you get this, and you didn't tell me about it?"

"Duck, I didn't know till two weeks ago what was going on." Probably today he'd still call me "Son." He'd say, "You wouldn't have been a damn thing if it hadn't been for me." Which I probably wouldn't have.

The funny thing about that watch business, when I left BOQ to go to the service school, it was the same time that Arthur Prettyman came in; that was Roosevelt's valet. In '44, he ran for the fourth term. So when I was going from the BOQ over to the service school, old Duck talked to the little old chief that made me wear those shoes. He said, "Chief Roe, we've got one guy here that's been through boot camp, OGU, he never pulled KP or guard duty since he's been in this man's Navy, and I thought everybody was supposed to do it."*

So he said, "Who?"

"That big one standing there."

So he walked up to me and said, "They tell me you haven't done any guard duty."

I said, "I've done everything I was asked to do in the Navy." I didn't tell them "Yes" or "No."

"Have you pulled KP or guard duty?"

I said, 'I've done everything, sir, I've been asked to do."

He said, "Something tells me you're sly." He walked up and punched me in the chest. He said, "I'm going to have a calf by you. You're going to pull some guard duty here, and plenty of it." While he was standing up there giving me hell, they called my

---

* OGU – out-going unit, that is, one in readiness for transfer to other duty.

name again to report to the officer of the day, then told me that I would go to another barracks and be master-at-arms at the service school.

I said, "Unh-unh, I won't pull no guard duty?" I didn't see him anymore till they called me down to Pearl Harbor, to go down and meet a ship and welcome some new draftees aboard. I walked down, and I was standing with my big .45 on, Bermuda shorts.

Paul Stillwell: You were an officer by then.

Mr. Arbor: I was an officer now, a big ensign. Who walked down the gangplank with orders in his arms but Chief Roe?

Paul Stillwell: I'll bet he was surprised.

Mr. Arbor: So I took his—he said, "Unh-unh."

I said, "That's all right. Forget about everything. I'm an officer now." I took his orders and sent them over there to the buses, lined them up. All I did was take him in my Plymouth and we'd have ridden along in front of the bus. I got behind the bus. When he got out, I took him into headquarters there like a messiah, you know. I wanted to bite him so bad, I didn't know what to do! I wanted him to let him know, "I am a man." You don't keep little petty things, but a learning process all along like that, I'm glad I didn't. That was a test of one's manhood, if he could be abused. He didn't call it abuse, because he had been in the Navy then some 30-something years.

Paul Stillwell: You showed you were a bigger man than he was.

Mr. Arbor: That's all I wanted to do, show him I was a bigger man than he was. When he had me across a barrel, and he was going to stretch the hide over my head. Just smoothed it over.

Paul Stillwell: Are there any memories you have of the curriculum—what you were studying during that time in boot camp?

Mr. Arbor: I just got sick of him reading the Articles of War to me, and "You will be subject to court-martial and will be shot," all that kind of stuff. I guess everything was to put the fear of God in you. Then, too, having come up like I did, under strict discipline through home, school, job, it wasn't hard for me to adjust, see. But these kids coming up now, they don't get any discipline at home, can't discipline them in school. They don't know what a church is, so where is he going to learn discipline? I believe everybody's son, humble or renowned, rich or poor, upon completion of high school, should spend at least 12 months in some branch of the service. I don't care whose child it is, especially a boy, so he can learn discipline, if nothing else.

Paul Stillwell: You were, obviously, one of the more educated in that group, probably one of the more mature and sophisticated. How did the others adjust in your company, let's say?

Mr. Arbor: See, now, in the group we went in, we all were about the same because we enlisted. We volunteered. They wouldn't accept you unless you were high school or better. We have an organization called World War II Black Naval Veterans of Great Lakes. Now in those conventions, you'll see those old-timers. They have to be over 65 to be in it, in that one. Now just at this last convention we had downtown here month before last, we were just counting the successful guys in there. We had six federal judges, 15 appellate court judges, PhDs no end. These were the guys who were up there in boot camp in 1942. That was the caliber of men you had. They selected 16 out of 70,000 such people.

Paul Stillwell: To go for the first officer training.

Mr. Arbor: Yes.

Paul Stillwell: How do you think you happened to be one of those 16?

Mr. Arbor: The good Lord and Charles Bamford, all I know.

Paul Stillwell: What had you done to impress Bamford?

Mr. Arbor: Well, when I got there, they put me in a leadership role. I guess the way I carried myself aboard ship, or when I was in the rec halls, when I got back on land. I just was always more of a conservative-type guy. That's the only thing, because I never had the slightest idea of applying for an officer. The height of my ambition was to be a quartermaster second class aboard that *Mason*. After that, I never thought about going any higher. If I could ever get up to be a chief quartermaster, that's why I was going to school all that time.

Paul Stillwell: You couldn't aspire to be an officer, because there weren't any.

Mr. Arbor: That was a thing of the past; they never heard of it. I never shall forget, somebody drew a picture of a black officer—didn't have it in our barracks. I don't know whether it was the battalion office—no, because I never went to a battalion office unless I was called. I'm trying to think where was that. It was just on a canvas. I don't know where I saw that picture up at Great Lakes, but to show you how stupid I was, I thought that was just a chief, of course, so it didn't faze me. Now Syl and Williams were telling me about that, and I said that was a chief. They said, "No, Jess, that was an officer. Didn't you see the gold braid on his cap?"

I said, "Didn't all chiefs have a gold braid?" I thought every officer, everybody that had on a cap was an officer. I didn't know. I guess they sent me that picture back. I'll show you my boot camp picture, when I came out of boot camp. The day I pulled off my boots, I saluted a chief, and I wondered why he didn't return the salute. Come to find out, he wasn't supposed to. I wasn't supposed to salute him. I didn't know that. That's the first day I came out of boot camp.

Did Syl and them show you the picture of that trip through John Lehman's office?

Paul Stillwell: No.

Mr. Arbor: That was aboard the USS *Kidd*; we went on a shakedown cruise.[*] These are some of the things I was on. Those people invited me out on that aircraft carrier, the *Carl Vinson*, in February. There's a cake they made in our honor. See Jesse Arbor's name up there first because—now this is Jerry Fireson here. He is the chief district federal judge for northern Illinois. He was in boot camp with them. These are some of the ones who didn't make it. That's Reginald Williams, that didn't make it. All these boys, except this one, he didn't get a master's, all these had master's or above.

Paul Stillwell: But you never had any idea why it was only 13 commissioned instead of 16?

Mr. Arbor: Never did. Williams believes that the reason why he didn't get it was because he was active in labor movements here during the CIO conventions and things, when they organized the steel workers out here in '37.[†] I was too.

Paul Stillwell: If that made a difference, they wouldn't have sent him to the school in the first place, you would think.

Mr. Arbor: See, they made a thorough FBI check on all of us. Of course, we didn't know it.

Paul Stillwell: This was before you were picked.

Mr. Arbor: Yes. Because I remember that friend of mine, who was the dean of Arkansas State College, wrote me after I got the commission, and wondered why the FBI was so inquisitive. And I got a letter from the Pullman Company, congratulating me, and told

---

[*] From 13 to 15 April 1982, the surviving members of the Golden Thirteen held a reunion on board the guided missile destroyer *Kidd* (DDG-993) at sea in the Atlantic. See PH2 Drake White, "Golden 13 Together Again," All Hands, August 1982, pages 8-11.

[†] In an interview in 1988, Williams indicated that he was told by Lieutenant (junior grade) John F. Dille in 1944 that he would not be commissioned because an FBI investigation had turned up the fact that he had been a labor organizer for railroad station redcaps. In an interview subsequent to that one, Dille did not recall giving such an explanation to Williams.

me the FBI—and all the neighbors around there on 62nd and St. Lawrence, where I was living, told me. That was after I had gotten out of the service. But they ran us through the mill. Pinkney was considered a radical, because he was working in some labor-organizing outfit—this is the way I understand it—in Atlanta.

Paul Stillwell: Before the war?

Mr. Arbor: Before the war. All this is in the '30s. Hathcock, the little musician, was recommended by Senator George of Georgia at that time, and he didn't get it.* Now he was head of a department at Clark College in Atlanta at that time.

Paul Stillwell: Did Alves have something like that in his background too?

Mr. Arbor: We never could find out what Alves was. The closest somebody said anything, that Alves said he was married and wasn't. Now that's the closest I found out what they said Alves was.

Paul Stillwell: Yes, but you'd think that was also something that could have been discovered before he was sent to the school.

Mr. Arbor: That's what I'm talking about, before they carried him through school, see. That's all I can understand. When I was down in Boston—see, he was from Providence, down in Rhode Island—I ran across some people who knew him. One of the fellows said, "I don't know why. It hurt Alves to his heart." But he said Alves, at that time, he had wife trouble; that was as near as he could think of. But other than that, I don't know anything, because all those people, you wouldn't want to be around a better group of fellows. Now, like Syl was a lawyer; he didn't know anything about seamanship. Alves was the best on seamanship. We'd all get around the table and work out seamanship.

---

* Walter F. George (Democrat-Georgia) served in the U.S. Senate from 22 November 1922 to 2 January 1957.

When it came to communication, I was in there, all around that. There wasn't such a thing as not knowing.

Paul Stillwell: So it was really a lot more cooperation than competition.

Mr. Arbor: It was 100% cooperation. Math—Reggie and George Cooper were good at that. Every course they had, we had an expert. Like Sam Barnes was there, he had a master's, and he was teaching when he came in there. So we had everything that way. Sublett and Baugh knew about boilers.

Paul Stillwell: What you didn't have was a lot of seagoing experience, really.

Mr. Arbor: Alves had that with five years.

Paul Stillwell: Really?

Mr. Arbor: With merchant marine.

Paul Stillwell: Then it's especially surprising that he didn't make it.

Mr. Arbor: That's what we wondered. He had experience in seamanship. He would teach us all the ship nomenclature, all the knots, and things like that. He could be practical. All of us in our field could be practical. Like Baugh and Sublett were proving automobiles and machines before they went into the Navy, so that fell right in their midst. They went down there and got the theory behind it. So we were just a unique bunch of fellows. I forget what Hair's specialty was, but it looked like they designed those courses just to fit us.* I talked to two or three of the instructors, one I see every time I go to the West Coast, and I think his name was Lowry. He was a legal officer. He didn't know Syl was a lawyer. They were both about the same age. He instructed us in naval law.

---

* James Edward Hair was a member of the Golden Thirteen; his oral history is in the Naval Institute collection. Before the officer training course he had seagoing experience as a quartermaster in the crew of a tugboat that operated out of New York City.

He just had gotten out of school, boot training in the Navy himself, so far as an officer. He said when he found out who he was teaching, said any number of days, he started not to come back.

Paul Stillwell: Who were your instructors? How were these people picked?

Mr. Arbor: I don't know how they picked them, but we didn't go to class; they came to us. We never left that building for anything but to eat.

Paul Stillwell: You were sort of kept off by yourselves.

Mr. Arbor: There's no "sort of." We were void of contact with anyone, except our instructors by day and ourselves at night.

Paul Stillwell: You couldn't you go on liberty.

Mr. Arbor: No, for about four or six weeks.

Paul Stillwell: How long was the whole course?

Mr. Arbor: Sixteen weeks.[*]

Paul Stillwell: Who were these instructors? Were they experienced people?

Mr. Arbor: In navigation . . .

Paul Stillwell: Sounds like your law guy wasn't.

Mr. Arbor: I know he wasn't.

---

[*] Actually more like ten weeks—from the beginning of January to mid-March 1944.

How to classify that experience—one night I was at the officers' club out at Guam, and one of the junior officers invited me over behind what we used to call that the bamboo curtain, where the senior officers were, and we had all the best whiskey. The Air Force, the Army, and the Marines out there couldn't get the whiskey the Navy had. So I would go over there at night. I don't know whether this was a Marine general, but he was the highest Marine officer on that island at that time, I understand. Lest I might be in error, I won't call this general's name, because I met him later on. But he heard that they had colored officers in the Navy. I said, "Yes, I'm living proof of that fact."

He said, "When I came from Guadalcanal back to [I forget now where he said he went] I heard they had you people in the Marine Corps. I said to myself, 'What the hell has this world come to now?' I got you people in the Marine Corps. After a while, they'll have Marine officers in there." He sat there, and he took his shot, and I got me a big one then. He said, "Oh, you're an officer."

I said, "Sir, two facts will be established before you break up this conversation. You've met one naval officer, one colored naval officer, and you've met your first colored man. Now, the Navy made me an officer, but I was a man when I came in the Navy."

He said, "I don't mean no harm."

I said, "That's all right." I got me another big shot, got up and walked on off.

He came by my barracks the next day. He said, "I want to apologize."

I said, "That's all right. The Navy, the Army, the Air Force, and the Marine Corps, all are just a microcosm of the society from which we come. If you didn't bring anything in, they can't make anything out of you." I said, "A few years from now, I would like to see you." I wanted to tell him, "I want to see what the hell you think." But I was trying to couch my—I don't care how mad I got, I always first, before I said anything, stop. I never let my sense of emotion rise up to cloud my thinking. If I had raised up, that would defeat the purpose.

Paul Stillwell: You couldn't afford to lose your temper in that situation.

Mr. Arbor: No. I had another situation where there was Hise, that little old boy from Rome, Georgia, Fetrow, myself. We used to get on those B-29 bomber runs, see, and go to Guam.* We weren't supposed to go, see. Our commanding officer told us, "You all can go if you want to, but if one of those damn things falls down out there, you ain't got no help." Just as long as you're on the island, they cut down that little old 21- to 22-year-old B-29 pilots. We'd make them drunk, "Come on a bombing run with us." We'd go up—I'm trying to figure out where we were. We ran into a bunch of Australian officers. I don't know whether it was Saipan, Tinian, or somewhere where we were over there with those little, old B-29 pilots, and we got over there.

All of the whiskey was on one of those Irish ships, as we called them over there. They were all officers, but weren't none of them Navy officers; there were Marine officers on there then, about eight or ten days after the invasion. By the time we got out, the little B-29 pilots warned us, "You have to show your ID card and all like that." So Joe Fetrow and myself, we went in with a B-29 pilot, saw them checking ID cards, and they'd hold your ID card and give you a permit to go aboard before you got off. That's what I understood they were doing it for. So they got to me. I took my ID card. I just had made jaygee. All three of us had made jaygee that same month. So when we go up the gangway, I said, "Joe, look here." It had on mine, "Jesse W. Arbor, lieutenant (j.g.), nationality: white." "Let me see yours, Joe." [Unclear] I said, "Let me see yours, Fetrow."

I showed them mine. They said, "My, oh, my, oh, my." Old Jess is passing for white. There were a lot of funny, comical things out there. The only time I felt bad on those islands before they were secured, or right after they were secured, and all those bodies that hadn't been completely buried or see the condition of kids and people. I've got a lot of those pictures and things that I took myself and developed. It just makes you hard, something like that. You get to the place where you don't have any compassion for anybody when you see all that stuff, and then you get off in retrospect and think about it. You say, "But for the grace of God, this could be my mama or sister or little grandchild or my child laying there," seeing little kids, all like that. That's what drove most of those people who drink or are crazy.

---

* The U.S. Army Air Forces' Boeing B-29 Superfortress was the most advanced bomber of World War II.

I ran across one old man, an old sailor, who taught me how to drink. He said, "Look, sailor. Don't you come out here and act like a damn fool and drink up all this whiskey. You can drink up all *my* whiskey, but you can't drink up all *the* whiskey. You've got to have good sense; otherwise, you wouldn't have made it as far as you have in this man's Navy. Everywhere you go in the Navy, they're going to throw a bottle in front of your face, everywhere you go. You can go to church and they're going to give you some wine. Before you take your first drink anywhere, at home or in the Navy, take you a tablespoon full of cod liver oil or olive oil, about five minutes before you start drinking. That whiskey will just run down through you and be fighting that olive oil, so you can drink all of these people under the table."

I said, "Chief, suppose I can't get the olive oil?"

He said, "I don't care where you go, they've got some GI butter. Get a stick of butter and eat it. If you can't get butter, just get plain old bacon grease or anything with grease in it, before you start drinking." And that's what I did, and I still do it today.

Paul Stillwell: You mentioned all these people that would comment to you that you could drink a lot without showing the effects. Did they know that from this guy who was tailing you?

Mr. Arbor: No.

Paul Stillwell: They knew it from watching.

Mr. Arbor: Yes. I don't know whether they knew it from him, because he asked me himself. There were no seats in those bars. I'd never walk up to a bar and do like this. I'd always try to get up near to the corner of this wall, or over there. I'd always get where I could observe everybody. I'd lay this arm up there. I'd step out. "Oh, that's all right." If someone would come up and bump me and step on my foot, that'd be a chance to apologize, something like that. I knew all that. Just start up a conversation. I've seen bartenders just pour it in there. They didn't measure anything. I'd tell them to always put nothing but ice in it because it was hot out there, and it would melt anyway. I'd let it melt down and sip it slow and never would move. I stood up at one place with a band there, that Liberace's brother was playing, George Liberace.* He was playing there that night on Guam. I stood up there and drank one fifth of Canadian Club by myself; of course, I had eaten almost a half a pound of butter before I went there.

Paul Stillwell: Oh, gosh!

Mr. Arbor: And it didn't feel any more than if I had had a couple of shots. The guy asked me, "Are you real, are you crazy, or what?" He said, "I was sober when you got here, and I've been drunk twice, and you still ain't drunk."

I said, "Well, I try to do everything in moderation." [Laughter]

I've been in positions where they want to try to test your intellectual prowess: how you are on a given subject. I told them right quick, "I'm a dummy. I don't know anything about anything. I just learned how to read and write after I got in the Navy." Pass it off as a joke, because nobody knows everything about any given subject. So I said, "You don't talk about religion or politics in this man's Navy, because everybody's got some kind of faith to live by, either Democrat or Republican or something. So whatever you are, we've all got to work together. I'm whatever you are. I'm adjustable." Don't try to put me in no category or back me in any corner. I'm working with everybody I come in contact with, and I bet you I'll get along with everybody. I won't knuckle down and kiss no asses, but I'll be a man.

I had a commanding officer when I was in Pearl Harbor. He was from New Orleans. He was a captain in the Army in World War I, and he was working in Honolulu. Of course, that was bombed, so he joined the Navy, and they made him a lieutenant commander. He was one of those kind like Armstrong, who knew just how the colored people act, and "I know everything about them, because I'm from New Orleans," and all like that. "I've been working with them on the docks down there," and that's how he got his. He was a nice, old guy, but he just couldn't keep that background out of his way of acting. But every night, we'd leave the officers' club, go to BOQ, have little old penny-ante poker games and things like that, a quarter, raise three times, a quarter, maybe

---

* Liberace was a flamboyant television entertainer in the 1950s.

a half-dollar. If I was going to play poker, I'd play it. If not, I'd just go down in my room and read or go to sleep. I had a little old radio. Every night he'd want me to, "Come on out, Mr. Arbor, and play a game or two with us."

I said, "Oh, well." I'd go up and play. I saw that they couldn't play poker. Just to be playing poker just to say I'm playing poker, I don't do that. I'm either going to win or lose. So I kept on telling them, "I just won't play this kind of game. If I'm going to lose $10.00, lose it. If I'm going to win ten, whatever I want, I do it all in one hand, get up, and go to sleep."

So after we played about two or three nights, all of them said, "That sounds right, Arbor." So the first night we played, I couldn't catch a hand against anybody but my CO, Grady Avant.* Sometimes I just turned my hand bottom-up. I'd say, "You can't beat this hand," and hid out on him. So for about a week or so, I wouldn't play. I wouldn't deal, because they'd figure I was slick, see. I might pass a little walking.

So this particular night, "Come on, Mr. Arbor. Let's play a little poker."

I said, "Boys, I like the way you play, because since I've been playing your style, I don't like that little old limited game anyway." That night I couldn't catch a hand on anybody but the man. They had another guy there. He said, "Look, Arbor, don't turn your hand over like that, because you're giving insight on my hand, or that hand, so just put it all in." So I'll never forget.

I said to myself, "I'm going to let the old man win a hand or two off me if there's any way possible, so he won't get mad." So I'll never forget, he had a pair of jacks. I had a pair of deuces showing, five cards. Going around, I said, "I'm just going to call, if it's in reason, so I know he's going to win it." Coming back around, I got three deuces. He had three jacks showing; I had three deuces showing.

So he said, "Well, Mr. Arbor, I guess I'm going to move you off here now, because I'm going to win one hand. I'm going to bet $5.00"

I said, "Well, Captain, you've been awful nice to me. This is your $5.00. Let's go $5.00" and I wouldn't raise.

He hit an ace; I hit a jack. But I got four deuces, and he got three jacks. He said, "I should have known there was a goddamned nigger in the woodpile." He just said it

---

* Lieutenant Commander Grady Avant, USNR.

unconsciously. So I just raked in the money. He didn't realize he said that. I raked it up, and I played two or three or four hands, and I got up and went on down the hall to my room.

After a while, I heard a knock on the door. He came in. He had a fifth of brandy. "Mr. Arbor."

"Come on in, Captain. I don't play no head up to nobody."

"No, I come down here to apologize."

I said, "For what? For losing the pot? I wouldn't apologize to you if I lost."

He said, "No, you didn't hear the expression I made."

I said, "You said 'pass,' didn't you?"

He said, "That's all you heard?"

I said, "That's all I was supposed to hear."

Interview Number 2 with Mr. Jesse W. Arbor
Place: Mr. Arbor's home in Chicago, Illinois
Date: Wednesday, 20 July 1988

Paul Stillwell: It's great to see you again, sir. I notice you've got some white new sideburns since I saw you the last time, and want to supplement the record that we made in October 1986. And one thought that comes to mind is to talk about your experiences in the Pullman cars. Mr. Williams said that he was prevented from becoming a naval officer because of his union-organizing activities for redcaps.* What was the status of the union among the Pullman car men back in those days?

Mr. Arbor: Well, see, in those days there were two unions in this city. There was the Pullman Company, which was national. It was the only national union for blacks in the '30s, headed up by A. Philip Randolph, who worked with the Pullman administration very closely. In other words, he was the top black union political man in the country. And they had one other small one here—the bartenders or something like that. I had been a member when I was going to school and working at the hotel there. If you waited tables, you had to belong to the bartenders' union. And with the Pullman Company, I just transferred my membership over there. But everybody all over recognized the Pullman Company, because it was backed by the Pullman porters—wasn't backed—it was sanctioned, I would say. And at that time there wasn't any airplanes, so Pullman was tops. When one came out of college in those days, if he didn't teach school, he went to the post office. My first [unclear] preacher, or lay minister, he had to go to the post office or the Pullman Company, because it was a better job than teaching school in those days.

Paul Stillwell: Well, evidently that union membership was not held against you.

---

* Lewis R. "Mummy" Williams was one of the three officer candidates who went through the training program but did not become officers. He was interviewed as part of the Naval Institute's oral history program, but his answers were often not credible. Redcaps were individuals who carried passengers' luggage in railroad stations.

Mr. Arbor: Well, when I went in the Navy, I had left the Pullman Company. You see, that's why I say we should have had this discussion about 40 years ago. I'm almost positive I'd left the Pullman Company, and I went back to the hotel.* And by the time I got back to the hotel, my draft number came up. So I was on record as having gone back to the hotel because I didn't want to work at the post office. I was not going to the steel mill or the stockyard, and I went on in the Navy.

But I remember very vividly, though—I must have left the Pullman Company then. Because when we got commissioned, the Pullman Company came out to interview me, and I ducked them.

Paul Stillwell: Why did you duck them?

Mr. Arbor: I don't know why. I just didn't want to be bothered with the Pullman Company or the hotel.

Paul Stillwell: Well, I think another difference, though, is that you were a union member but not an organizer.

Mr. Arbor: I often thought about that. When I was going to school, in those days after we got in the union out at the hotel, they raised our salary to $37.50 a month—raised it. [Chuckle] And got paid the first and 15th, not every two weeks.

I was on the way from the hotel, I was walking down Hyde Park Boulevard, and I met a bunch of kids from the international house over there at the University of Chicago. They were having a meeting at Jackson Park. This was in 1940, and they wanted somebody to speak. I came to find out they were members of the Rising Sun, a Japanese organization, some kind of social organization at the university. And so [unclear] someone said, "See if you can make this speech. You've got the gift of gab."

I said, "How much?"

"Forty dollars."

---

* In the 1930s Mr. Arbor had begun working as a doorman for the Chicago Beach Hotel, at 51st and Lake in the Hyde Park area of the city.

I said, "Yes." I wasn't making $40.00 a month then. So I went on over to the park. And I took the thing they handed me. On my way out I was reading it. They had given me $40.00, and the paper they gave me had something in it, "After this present conflict is over, we the members of the Rising Sun will democratize the United States"—something to that effect. I can't remember it verbatim.

Paul Stillwell: Had the war already started by then?

Mr. Arbor: No. See Pearl Harbor didn't happen until December 1941.

Paul Stillwell: So this is their war with China they were talking about?[*]

Mr. Arbor: I don't know what they were talking about. And didn't care; I had $40.00. [Chuckle] So we went down to the park, and I was on the stump, and after a while here came the police, and they started throwing salt and pepper. And I just took off.

In about a week I met another group over in Washington Park, got out on the stump there. Whatever they wrote it, I'd say it.

Paul Stillwell: Whether you believed it or not.

Mr. Arbor: I didn't believe any of it. But the FBI was trailing all those folks. I was just after the money. I didn't write anything.

Paul Stillwell: It's interesting that the FBI investigation didn't turn that up on you.[†]

Mr. Arbor: After looking at that in relation to the FBI investigation, I think about how in the world could they be so exact on things like that and couldn't find Howard Hughes

---

[*] Japan and China had been at war since 1937. The Japanese euphemistically referred to the conflict as the "China Incident."
[†] During the process in which black enlisted personnel were being screened for officer training, the Federal Bureau of Investigation did background checks on the candidates.

flying all over the country.* They'd go to one island and the entire hotel and come back to California, all of southern California then go to Las Vegas and build a hotel, get on the Spruce Goose and fly it, and the FBI couldn't find him.† I just can't figure that out.

Paul Stillwell: I don't think they had the same motivation.

Mr. Arbor: No, no. [Laughter] They knew where he was all the time.

But, see, I never was a union organizer per se—I was a member because you had to be to work in the city, pull two jobs. And they were the best ones I could get. Even lawyers—if they didn't have enough money to open up an office, a number of lawyers went out to the post office.

Paul Stillwell: Did the Communist Party approach you at all?

Mr. Arbor: No. If they did they didn't identify themselves as such. Because a lot of times, you'd go over and get them at the speakers' bureau periodically, I don't know, religious or what. "I don't know about this; this is your show. Get the money up front, so if I have to run, I can take off. It's your program." As long as they didn't get too radical. I wouldn't want to take it home with me. Wherever they make a speech or took off running, I wouldn't want to be there.

Paul Stillwell: How many groups, or how many times were you approached for this kind of thing?

Mr. Arbor: I would say at least a dozen times.

---

* Howard R. Hughes Jr. (1906-1976) was an American businessman, aviator, movie producer, and philanthropist. During his latter years he became a recluse who often moved around to various locations.
† The Hughes H-4 Hercules was a large flying boat designed to ferry troops across the Atlantic in World War II. It was made almost entirely of wood and earned the nickname "Spruce Goose." Its only flight was on 2 November 1947. At that time Howard Hughes was still very much in the public eye. Arbor's reference was tongue in cheek.

Mr. Jesse W. Arbor, Interview #2 (7/20/88) – Page 73

Paul Stillwell: So do you have the idea that your name was passed around as someone who would do this?

Mr. Arbor: You know you got in circles. I wasn't married and I was on the hotel door at the time. I never meant any strangers, anything like that. I was always put myself in a position where those people would be. At the speakers' bureau, you see. Hang around there, didn't drink, didn't smoke. I was a good boy. So had a common cause, they'd think I was better than I was. So [unclear], or we were discreet as to what I could do. No matter what you told them, I'd have to twist around it somewhere where I wouldn't be saying, "yes, yes," all the time for everything.

Paul Stillwell: What was their motivation in having a black man make these speeches?

Mr. Arbor: I've often wondered about that because any—I've never—but the audience, why, they were, unless there were one or two students, they were black. I don't know. I just guess having my big mouth that would talk.

Paul Stillwell: Unless they were trying to foment some kind of rebellion and—

Mr. Arbor: I don't see how they could foment one using the material and the times. Now, if war had broken out, see, because I never would have pulled it off. I'd heard the news, per se, but, I mean the war about the islands and things like that but no bombs—that didn't happen until December of '41.

Paul Stillwell: So this is a year or a year and a half earlier.

Mr. Arbor: Yeah, a year and a half or maybe 18 months, or something like that, before. But I wasn't interested in whatever they were doing or planning on doing after this turmoil. I didn't even know what—I didn't know what it was all about until after Pearl Harbor. I was at the hotel. Because I remember that was December 7, the first naval officer I remember seeing dressed up.* I was a doorman out there then, and he came through the lobby, his mother just crying. He was home on leave. I remember him saying very vividly, "Oh, mother, don't worry about it. They'll never have to call out the Army. We'll have this thing wrapped up in 90 days."

Paul Stillwell: How wrong he was.

Mr. Arbor: And that was on a Sunday afternoon. I never will forget. And that Monday I didn't have to go to the employment until 3:30 that afternoon. I went over to a Twelfth Street store and bought me a new suit and a pair of shoes and sat down and read his famous speech that "Day of Infamy." And I don't think I wore that suit but two or three times. [Laughter] By that time, it was too small for me.

Paul Stillwell: Was there any connection between Pearl Harbor and buying a new suit?

Mr. Arbor: No, I—see all the boys—I was the last single man in Draft Board 7. All the boys were gone, and I was going back to the road. That was because the head of the Pullman Company, told me, said, "See if you'd stayed with the Pullman Company, we might have been able to save you." Of course they hauled in soldiers and sailors, so I was going back to the Pullman Company. I never did make it back there.

Paul Stillwell: Because your buddy got taken, so he couldn't protect you anymore.

Mr. Arbor: Umm-hmm. That's it. [Laughter] I couldn't get back to the Pullman, and my buddy couldn't help me any at all.

Paul Stillwell: Were any of these speeches that you made so radical that they suggested overthrowing the government?

---

* On Sunday, 7 December 1941, Japanese carrier planes attacked and heavily damaged American warships at the naval base at Pearl Harbor, Hawaii. The U.S. Congress declared war on Japan the next day after hearing President Franklin D. Roosevelt make an address.

Mr. Arbor: The only reference I can remember was one that I made when we threw the salt and pepper in this policeman's eyes. When they did; I was on the way out. After this, if there's a conflict or turmoil, we're going to democratize America"—something to that effect. What was sensitive in most of the speeches, I wish I'd kept a copy of those. I didn't. Unh-uh. I'd have it in my mind; I'd just write it out. You know, since then, as soon as I got out of the service, I didn't go back to those speeches at all, because they did not seem to have any—that I was really jealous for the percentage. And they didn't have the interest of an audience; you would find it hard   I came to find they just had a think tank of writers sit down and writing speeches for any occasion. First thing they want to know how to apprise the audience, whether the age group, educational background, and social or political. And they'd just reach in and draw a speech for any occasion. Just fill in the dates and the salutations.

Paul Stillwell: So you were sort of like President Reagan. You just—*

Mr. Arbor: [Laughter] I just did that with a writer of speech, a pertinent one.

Paul Stillwell: You were just a performer.

Mr. Arbor: That's so. I just needed me a good writer of speeches.

I had—wasn't about the other brothers [unclear section] because he was parading along the faculty there, his speech was in California. He used to travel all the time. He used to tell me four or five [unclear section] said I could make money at it. I said, "No, you've got to have something back there."

He said, "You can talk just so long that you had to sit down and think sometimes."

Paul Stillwell: When did you find out about the FBI investigation that was done on you?

---

* Ronald W. Reagan served as President of the United States from 20 January 1981 to 20 January 1989. He was in office at the time of this interview.

Mr. Arbor: When I came back here from—I got "Greetings" from Uncle Sam. I just took off for Mexico and went down and stayed.

Paul Stillwell: But wasn't there another one, though, leading up to you being in officer training?

Mr. Arbor: Oh, yes, but I don't know why they overlooked that. The only time that I was aware that the FBI had been looking for me is when I did report for draft before I enlisted in the Navy. The next time I knew anything about it was after I got my commission. And they talked to my mother, and they went out and wanted to talk to my dad, and everybody in town. They wanted to know when I was in high school Some of it I didn't hear about until I got out of the service.

Paul Stillwell: What was your reaction when you found out that you'd been investigated?

Mr. Arbor: I was beginning to wonder what the hell had I done [laughter] that would have them do all of that. Then I started taking stock of myself and said, "Oh, well, you hadn't pushed any little chickens in the water and hadn't robbed a bird's nest, or anything like that, so you were just about as clean as you could be." I didn't feel that this little episode was something they could hold against me. I was just a conduit out there for suggesting, or organizing, or actually putting anything into effect, because they surely knew that I was being paid.

Paul Stillwell: Did you resent the fact that you'd been investigated?

Mr. Arbor: No. Unh-uh. Because in one's life you'll be investigated by somebody constantly, so you just learn to live with it as a fact of life. And I've always tried to live in such a way that I can look anybody in the eye. Wake up, I go to the mirror and brush my teeth every morning, and look myself in the eye. If I can look myself in the eye and say that I mistreated no one yesterday, that's my yardstick.

Paul Stillwell: Well, you did have a few schemes, such as that thing with the grapefruit.*

Mr. Arbor: [Laughter] Well, one has to have a little side pleasures occasionally. Keeps from getting in the rut. [Laughter] That's part of the growing process.

Paul Stillwell: We didn't talk too much before about your enlisted time. I'd like to get some more of that on the record, if we could please. What do you remember about boot camp?

Mr. Arbor: Well, that was interesting. I guess I led a charmed life all the way through the Navy.

When I went down, reported down to Fort [unclear]. I think that was on a Monday, yes. Was a boot there from Chicago—I didn't know any of them. But one guy in there knew me—and in an unpleasant way. He was the only one in the group that had had any ROTC experience. He was the oldest in the group, so they gave him the orders to take us up to Great Lakes. I didn't know he knew me, but he knew me and hated me.

When we got up to Great Lakes, they hadn't any running water or anything in the barracks; they put them up so fast—no sidewalks, no anything.† So they took us over about Wednesday to get our uniforms. They gave us double-soled shoes, dungarees, undress jumper, and a peacoat, and that little $5.00 bag they gave you with shaving cream, the toothpaste, and everything. Gave you $5.00 and you go down to the other end, and they take the $5.00. Called it a flying five then.

By the end of the week, this boy—I [unclear section]—he was so clumsy, he couldn't keep cadence, although he could call. By the end of the week I knew how to call cadence. But that little old guy was—we called him Duckbill. His name was Arthur Collins from Kansas City. They put him in our company, and one guy [unclear] and he was fresh out of ROTC. But he weighed about 100 pounds and made him right guide. And my name Arbor, and the tallest thing was in front. He took a liking to me. He said,

---

* In his first interview Arbor described rubbing grapefruit on his skin to cause a flare-up and thus avoid having to go back to duty in the Pacific.
† Within the Great Lakes Naval Training Station, north of Chicago, Camp Robert Smalls was the site of training for black recruits. It was named for an escaped slave who captured the Confederate steamer *Planter* during the Civil War and turned her over to the U.S. Navy. Arbor enlisted in September 1942.

"Hey, as big as you are, normally you ought to be able to do better than that. You'll land up there in front."

I said, "Duck," . . .

He said, "Shut up because I'm going to make something out of you tonight." We were sleeping in the hammocks. Arbor, Downes, Collins, McCarver, Brown, Brussard. Collins was supposed to lay down. I used to fall out—all you had to do like BAM on the floor. We were sleeping in the hammocks and didn't know how to get out. Once you got in there—so Duck eased me out and took me into the head. He said, "Big Man," hit that thing, and BAM. [Unclear] So everybody laughed. They thought I had fallen out of the bed. He said, "Come on, we're going in the head." He took me in the head and said, "Left, right, left, right. To the rear, march."

He said, "Oh, dummy," and he kept me in there for about three hours until he said, "Now I'm going to tell the commander that you called cadence. I'm right there by you. You can hear good, can't you?"

I said, "Yeah." [unclear]

Now I asked, "When I say, 'To the rear,' what the hell am I going to say to get them to go back?" When they would get too close, Duck whispered, "To the rear, march." Duck said, "This is good."

I got to be apprentice company commander there. I didn't have to stand watch. You don't pull guard duty always in boot camp nor KP. When I got out of boot camp I went to OGU.* They made me master-at-arms. Published the watch list—I didn't put myself on watch list. When I went to the service school, they put me in charge of the barracks, [unclear]. All the time I almost made guard duty, they had a little old chief there—looked like a zebra. Used to take those firemen, like firemen in World War I, who knew nothing about military procedure and make them as a role model down there so put him in charge of the master-at-arms, or something. I don't know what he was in charge of, had something to do with the master-at-arms.

But, anyway, the word got out that I had been in there 16 weeks and never stood guard duty. So when we were coming back from liberty after we got out of boot camp,

---

* OGU – out-going unit, those designated for reassignment.

we had to go to OGU, where he was in charge. So he walked up to me one day, captain sitting in the back.

"Your name is Arbor?"

"Yes, sir."

He punched me in the chest, said, "I understand you haven't pulled KP or guard duty since you've been in this man's Navy. Who in the hell do you think you are?"

"I've been in the Navy, always keeping my mouth shut." Stood at attention.

He says, "Well, so you're in OGU now, and I'm in charge. I'm going to have a calf by you when you're here." I stood there. He says, "Shove off." Called this chief passing on to the enlisted man: "Get his name and put him on the dog watch tonight!"

That's all right. I understood it.

Go over to the barracks and time I got back from chow: "Now hear this, now hear this. The following named sailors lash up your seabags in seagoing fashion and report to the officer of the day. Arbor, Jesse W." BAM!

Going out to go to service school that was in another barracks. I told myself, [chuckle] "Well, those [unclear section]—as long as he went, I'm not going to stand guard duty." And I moved out. I didn't see—Chief Ross was his name.

Paul Stillwell: He was a white man?

Mr. Arbor: No.

Paul Stillwell: He was a black?

Mr. Arbor: Umm-hmm. So I didn't see him anymore until I was on the way out the gate, and I waved at him.

He shook his head: "I'll run across you somewhere in this man's Navy. I get around."

I said, "Yes, sir."

The next time I saw him was when I came back to Great Lakes for officers' indoctrination. I didn't know what happened to him or nobody else. Later I was at Pearl

Harbor. They sent me down to the docks to welcome in a group of new sailors. Who was in charge of the bunch? Chief Ross. I was standing there, shorts on, .45 wrapped around, my ensign bars on. He stepped off the gangplank and gave me the orders.

Paul Stillwell: And his jaw dropped.

Mr. Arbor: He looked at me. I said, "Welcome aboard, Chief."

I checked him in, gave him the muster. I put them on one of those cattle trucks; I wouldn't let him get on the cattle truck. I had a brand-new '40 Plymouth. I put him in the Plymouth with me and drove on over to where the man was supposed to stay.

I said to myself, "I'm going to ride along and see if he's going to open up the conversation.

He sat there.

"Well, Chief," I said, "time brings about a change, doesn't it?"

"Yes, sir, it sure does."

I said, "You don't have to 'sir' me." I wanted to start off with a joke. "At ease." I said, "You are strictly Navy. You were in the Navy almost before I was born." I said, "I do you the highest respect, and I intend to give it. Now that I'm an officer, that does not change."

Paul Stillwell: He was very relieved.

Mr. Arbor: Umm-hmm. And I was a bigger man than he was. That's always been my philosophy as I get old too.

Now all through my enlisted career I never—I guess some guys go out on this "damn Navy so-and-so," and so on and so on. I asked them, "What did you bring to the Navy to build on?" I said, "I can't kick the Navy. Every time a promotion was due me, I got it." I said, "But I [unclear]. Whatever they told me to do, I did it. That's the name of the game." I said, "Now, what did you—what did you fall short?"

"Just because I didn't do . . . "

"That's it. And you expect them to reward you just because you didn't do what they said?" [unclear] I said, "Every one of us in this Navy volunteered. I know I did. You volunteered for something, and then you want to change the rules? You want to get out? If you're a big enough fool, they'll put you out. It's like somebody sitting in the theater behind you tickling you in an ear with a feather. They're not hurting you, but they won't let you enjoy the picture. That's what you're doing. You're tickling your own self in the ear. You're not the only one in here. Everywhere you look you see a boy with a white hat on. He's having the same trouble as you have and enjoying life just like you are. You may be miserable." I told him, "Right now if you don't have anything to take to the Navy, the Navy can't give you a damn thing. If at times on your job here, while in the Navy, every time you see your superior, and you're crying the blues, anybody'd get sick of it. None of us are happy all the time. But every time you meet somebody and you're crying the blues, something wrong with you."

Paul Stillwell: Now, who was this fellow you were telling this to?

Mr. Arbor: Oh, that's my spiel as I go around talking to these kids in the state.

Paul Stillwell: I see.

Mr. Arbor: And in recruiting, it's kind of hard for an old man to talk to an 18- or 19-year-old boy. Now they got nice young—we are the last resort—it's just like planting a flower in a garden. When it's time to pluck the flower, harvest the fruits, something like that, you report back here for months. They say, "This man made so and so, and so and so." The way I like to do is like you look at—you've got one or two boys. They are slightly undecided what they want to do: "Oh, I'm not going to Vietnam," or "I'm not going to—" That's all you could hear. These kids don't know about Vietnam, but they hear their older brothers and cousins talk about it. "I'm going to do something. I'm going to school. I don't know."

I'd say, "You should start to make up your mind now. You're in the ninth grade." I've got a grandson. He's going in the ninth grade now. I told my son, "I practice what I preach." So I did with my grandson. Of course, my son is 38 years old. [Unclear] My grandson will be 13 in January. I said, "You've got to make up your mind what you want." Nobody taught him that. Now several years he was coming out of high school, and his uncle said, "I would like for you to talk to [unclear]. I said, "I'm older than you. I'm older than your daddy. I'm going to send a young, fresh naval recruiter and take you to dinner. And I won't tell him why or nothing. And I'm going to leave [unclear section]. We're going to support [unclear]"

I said, "Tell you what I'm going to do. I'm going to take both of you to a meeting." And I'd tell him about Great Lakes. [Unclear section]

We were all sitting there, and when they introduced me, he looked up. I came back and sat down and didn't say a word to him yet. On the way home he picked up the conversation: "You mean to tell me you were an officer in the Navy way back there then?"

I said, "Way back there then."

Paul Stillwell: One of the first.

Mr. Arbor: So the next two or three days his dad brought him by for dinner. I showed him the boot camp picture, and he had seen it. And the next month, he's at Great Lakes now. And his old man says, "It's the greatest thing that ever happened, because he was not going to college. He said he wasn't. He didn't have a job, and he was getting around these various gangs. I had a call from him. He's out in San Diego now. Thanked me for everything, for not letting me know who I was.

Paul Stillwell: Why was that important?

Mr. Arbor: The shock that—now, see, nobody believes anything when they're 13 to around 17-18 years old. Nobody believes anything. You know everything. I knew everything.

Paul Stillwell: I've got a son who thinks he knows everything.

Mr. Arbor: That's the problem in life that we just don't believe that we were that big a fool. We were. We just weren't that great ourselves.

So every kid now, either humble or renowned, or rich or poor, wants to be a part of something. It's up to us to try to steer him in the right direction. You can't push him too hard. Otherwise, he'll rebel at most anything. But if we can keep nudging him and pushing him in the right direction, 90% of them will take at least 60% of what you tell them. None of us are going to take 100% of anything.

Paul Stillwell: How much of that type work do you do now?

Mr. Arbor: I do quite a bit of it voluntarily.

Now I'd like to have the setting where I don't have to beat the bushes. Because I'm too old to run around or play basketball or jump. I sit down and talk with them. That's why I was trying to get this boy that just made chief. And he [unclear]. I said I didn't use him. [Unclear section—my son—my daughter's finishing high school so that has he has entrée to a lot of boys that he wouldn't if he didn't have that little bit of help, see.

She's always saying, "Dad, let's go to this school."

Well, he'd go ahead and ferret them out, and we could take him around and show him that Navy wasn't so bad. Now, the Air Force and the Marines—the Air Force is killing the Navy in this city. With this and that, you know, freshly starched, first or second lieutenant now; he looks so young. If you squeeze his nose, milk would run out of his mouth. He's so young and tempting. And he's talking to them, "Man, you could fly."

Everybody wants to ride a motorbike or fly. But now they're putting up this naval aviation program now, and I can talk quite a—but I always insist that you be good in hard sciences. I said, "If you're not, [hissing noise.] I say, "Try to maintain a B average or better. Nobody wants a dummy up there flying this plane. You're going to fall down and kill yourself and somebody on the ground. You've got to be able to read those various instruments up there and think quickly."

That is the best approach I see in recruiting. You don't go down there and promise them, "I'm going to make you admiral in ten months." You come to the Navy, and the Navy will make—" Look at me," and I tell them how long it took me to get there. Hard work, which most kids don't know a damn thing about. They have no chores at home. Like when my boy was coming up here, I said, "Now, as long as you are here, there are certain chores you must do. One of them is mop the kitchen and the basement at least twice a week. Every day's not necessary because you can't mop the other parts of the house [unclear]." I said, "You can rake all the leaves in the fall and cut all the grass all summer." I love him.

"Glad to do that, Dad," he said. [Unclear] nary a leaf. That's how it goes. And he did. I had to keep prodding him and kicking his butt around sometimes. But he learned how to be responsible for something. Sometimes he failed to do that, and I'd make him go over it. Then I'd reward him after he got 16 or 17 years old. I let him try out the car some Friday nights. That was his pay. And I'd give him a couple of bucks to take someone to a show or something like that. But that's the same thing in life. That's what I tell these kids in the neighborhood. You've got to do what you're told. You have to face responsibilities and accept them.

Paul Stillwell: Your parents instilled that in you, I'm sure, back in Arkansas.

Mr. Arbor: No, they didn't instill it; they kicked it into me.

Paul Stillwell: [Laughter]

Mr. Arbor: And they would tell you once. If they told you twice, you should have done it yesterday, not today. Whatever he told you to do today, if he told you to do it twice, you should have done it yesterday.

Modern fathers and mothers try to give junior and sister everything we wish we had. I could have got [unclear] you know, except you turn that bottom side up one time [spanking sound with hands] and, "Now go do it."

Paul Stillwell: What other values did you get from your parents?

Mr. Arbor: The greatest thing that I can fall back on is to always follow instructions. Never beg off and say, "Yes, I know what you want," unless you understand what the person who's paying you wants done. Don't go off half-cocked. If you don't understand, ask 1,000 times before you act. Then if you do what they say, and it's wrong, they know that they told you the wrong, and your conscience is always clear. Always put your best foot in front of you. Never go off half-cocked. And never do anything to anybody that you wouldn't want done to you. And you couldn't be more precise than that. And I tried to teach it to mine.

Paul Stillwell: What role did religion play in your family when you were growing up?

Mr. Arbor: Always. Always. Every morning everybody would come to the breakfast table and the old man prayed and blessed the food. Every Sunday morning before breakfast, everybody would sit around and then read some scripture in the Bible; they'd have prayer. That was every morning until the last kids left home. Started with one kid, the first one—no, he died before the last two left home, up until he died. He read the Bible. We'd have to get down and let him pray. He'd get up and go to the far end of the table after he'd blessed the food. And Mama would serve his plate first. He'd come around and then go to church. We had to go to church. Except when we got 16 to 17 years old, and you didn't want to go to church, if you were there he'd say, "Yeah, you'll go. You don't stay here." He said, "If it won't help you, it certainly won't hurt you. Sit up there and go to sleep, but you'll be in church. You won't be out doing the devilment."

Religious—we all had to go to—we never went to a public school a day in our lives, none of us. He got up the money somehow. He said, "I want you to have what I didn't have. They didn't have any schools like this when coming up. He got to the fourth grade; he graduated. That's as high as it went.

He was the first generation of kids going to school after slavery. "That's as far as I could go. But you've got a chance to go on through high school." And we found out kids went to college, and his first son went to college, he couldn't—[unclear section] I went to college, and I was number seven. And his chest began to pop open. And his brother had all girls; Papa had all boys. And he took to me because I always had a lot of mouth, and he tried to trade one of his daughters for me. [Laughter] But after I came right through there for sophomore year in college. They'd see my name in the *Defender*, playing football and all like that.* My uncle just got down and cried almost: "Lord, Lord, I wish you were my son." [Unclear section] He told my dad, "I give up two of my daughters for you."

"We don't trade. That's like that old slavery times stuff."

"Just don't look like it's fair. So you have ten boys and two girls; I got ten girls." And the boys all young." He says, "Why couldn't I have one boy? Tell me."

I said, "You got one."

He said, "Look like all you boys right along together. Four boys, one girl, four boys, and one girl. I'd like one boy more than six girls."

Paul Stillwell: I'd like to hear more about your football playing when you were at Arkansas AM&N.† How good were you?

Mr. Arbor: Well, I had to be the best because I was the only right tackle they had, so I was worth—no, I'm kidding, no. See I never played high school football, and I knew I had to—and I had a brother who'd been there; this was his fourth year. And at that time, it didn't belong to—those colleges hadn't joined the Southwestern Conference. So you played until you left, or graduated, or got kicked out—one of the two.

My brother had finished high school then and went into college. So I think Elmer had been playing in there, look like me about 20 years when I got there, and he was six years old older than I was. [Laughter]

So when I went there, the coach—I don't know what they did in the recruiting season—got there and hauled us [unclear] recruiting coach. So they kept me there until after Elmer's brother had finished high school. They put us in to work. I weighed like 186 pounds then. So when they came back, I wasn't a quarterback and right end. I was the smallest man on the team. So they called me "Elmer's baby brother," so they started calling me "Baby."

---

* The *Chicago Defender* was a black newspaper with national circulation.
† The institution is now the University of Arkansas at Pine Bluff; during Arbor's time as a student it was Arkansas Agricultural, Mechanical and Normal (AM&N) College.

Now, I didn't know tackle from guard, or quarterback from quartermaster, or nothing. I just didn't know—just dumb, that's all. Because they didn't have anything at our high school except basketball. So this school then told me how to—showed me how to get down. Didn't tell me in a sentence, because I was too dumb to get down, and they didn't want to overload the wagon. So finally they gave me a playbook. Not a play book—four or five sheets of paper with some plays on them to memorize—with X's and 0's down there. So the captain of the team—I met him last week out at Atlanta [phonetic]—he took me aside and said, "What position are you going out for?"

I said, "What position's open?"

He said, "Well, for your brother's position because he's so old and lazy, he ain't going to play."

I said, "What position is that?"

He said, "Tackle."

So I went out for tackle. And another guy—it was his second year, and left tackle, so my brother was right tackle, so they put me scrimmaging in his position. And then put us in the same room together—had three boys to a double room. My brother was in the top bunk; other boy had springs on the bottom [unclear] Montana [unclear].

They were playing deadly in those days. Shoot, on the line you'd think they were prizefighters. You would end up banging up your mouth, lead you all over the lot, kneed, and pass by you. All these marks on my leg down there, my own brother put them on there in scrimmage. Pass by and cut you up with those cleats. And pick up a handful of sand—come up and throw sand up your nose, mouth, everything.

So I went out for my brother's position. They put him on a separate team and put him on the other side, so I would face him. And I was so much stronger than he was, and faster, I just kept him on his butt, knocked him over. He got smart. He started whipping me with his cleats.

So I asked him one day—I was in the shower with this bleeding and legs aching. So I asked him, "Why do you keep kicking on me on my legs? Pick on somebody else. I'm your brother."

He said, "Tell so-and-so is on the field [unclear]. Get on the other side then."

I said, "Big boys over there."

He said, "They're no larger than I am. Get over there."

I said, "I've got to stay over where the coach tells me."

So one of the other boys had been trailing along and overheard the conversation. He came, and I said, "You stay right there. That's the only spot open on this team. They don't carry no spares." There were 15 men on the whole team, including the coach.

He said, "You play 60 minutes or nothing. Your brother ain't going to play 60 minutes." He said, "In a little while he's going to get tired. And they ain't gonna run him off the campus. They'll run you off. Then where you gonna eat?"

I said, "Oh, no. I've got to play tackle." I made the team. They started write-ups and sent them to the *Pittsburgh Courier*.* [Unclear section] "That old boy's doing all right." [Laughter] So that's how I got through college.

And then summertime—when I first got on the railroad—I started—in the summertime I was [unclear] football. Basketball they'd get on the railroads. They'd see to that. They'd [unclear] but all of us had scholarships.

Paul Stillwell: How was it that you were so much stronger than your brother?

Mr. Arbor: Younger, that's all. And he knew how to play football; I didn't. That's the way he was when he got there. And after I was there two or three years, I got lucky and knew I could take chances. Because he was larger than I was, older, and knew the game. After I learned how to keep from getting all kicked up, I started putting the punishment out instead of taking it. And I got a little lazy too.

Paul Stillwell: How well did your teams do?

Mr. Arbor: Let me see, '32, we were just talking about that last week. We ended up, I would say, a 50-50 team. That's what Red [unclear] was telling me. He said since then—because we got our uniforms, we—Skip Hazard had made some connection with the

---

* The *Pittsburgh Courier* was a black newspaper that published from 1907 to 1966. In the 1930s it was one of the top black papers in the United States.

Chicago Cardinals.* Because he met somebody when he was going to Northwestern University to get his master's. He met somebody that he arranged to get those old uniforms from Chicago Cardinals, and that's what we were using. We'd get new jerseys but not [unclear]. But those trunks, shoulder pads—we got jerseys and jockeys new. That's all. Shoes, pads, trunks, and whatever—they'd throw trunks and things in the laundry. I think about the shoes. If they fit, they were yours. And so many of those boys had athlete's foot. I was lucky; I didn't ever get it. I don't know why anybody would have known not jockey straps and shoes. It would be like using somebody's dentures. [Laughter]

And I came to find out that most all of those colleges—they were doing the same thing, an entrée to some of these professional teams. And some of those state colleges were using the uniforms from the white state colleges—and books. But we were high class; we had professional uniforms.

Paul Stillwell: How serious was the approach from the Cardinals for you to play for them?

Mr. Arbor: The only reason why I didn't—I believe until the day I—I didn't make the Cardinal team because I couldn't afford to give up the job at the hotel to go try out and miss making the team. Because I believe until this day I could have made it. But I just couldn't afford to lose my job back there in those days. They were too hard to get.

Paul Stillwell: I think you told me the Cardinals offered you $500.00.

Mr. Arbor: Five hundred dollars. They were just too hard to get.

I wish now, looking back on hindsight, I had taken—I could have said I tried. That's the only thing I feel. But I actually believe my knowledge of football in college—I don't care how rough it would have been in those days, I would have known how to dish it out and take it.

---

* The Chicago Cardinals were in the National Football League for many years before moving to St. Louis prior to the 1960 season. In 1988 the team moved to Phoenix and became the Arizona Cardinals.

The worst thing is to sit back in retrospect—I didn't try.

Paul Stillwell: Well, not many black men were given the opportunity like that.

Mr. Arbor: Oh, that's the part that hurts. I don't think they'd have but one or two—Duke Slater and who else?

Paul Stillwell: Certainly not very many.

Mr. Arbor: I'm trying to think, say Marion Motley, and I'm trying to think but I can't—

Paul Stillwell: I thought he was a little later than that.

Mr. Arbor: Yes, Motley was. I think it was Duke Slater.[*]

Paul Stillwell: Yes, he was in the '20s, as I recall.

Mr. Arbor: Duke?

Paul Stillwell: Yes.

Mr. Arbor: Oh, yeah, yeah. I can't remember anybody else with the Cardinals. Duke and Motley. And I was a walk-on. I wasn't invited.

Paul Stillwell: What do you mean you were in a walk-on?

Mr. Arbor: You just walk through the gate when they were practicing.

---

[*] Fred W. "Duke" Slater played in the National Football League from 1922 to 1931. In two of his seasons, 1927 and 1929, he was the only black player in the NFL. Marion Motley started his professional career with the Cleveland Browns of the All-America Football Conference in 1946. There were no black players between 1931 and 1946.

Paul Stillwell: And they were impressed enough with you from a tryout?

Mr. Arbor: Umm-hmm. Agent? Who was that?

Paul Stillwell: [Laughter] No, you didn't have an agent.

Mr. Arbor: No, no, no, no. Used to love to hang around over there at that park. And I remember the first time I went to a workout. They didn't give me a uniform. It was summertime. I wore just a T-shirt and a pair of blue shorts or khaki shorts.

Paul Stillwell: Where did they have the tryout?

Mr. Arbor: Over at Comiskey Park.[*]

Paul Stillwell: I guess they played there for a long time before they went to Soldier Field.

Mr. Arbor: Umm-hmm. I know they practiced over there. And I turned out maybe four or five times over there. And when they got ready to go to camp, I just couldn't go.

Paul Stillwell: They actually offered you a contract?

Mr. Arbor: If I made the team. I think that's the way they did it most. In those days you didn't sign coming out of college and sign for X number of dollars. [Unclear section] You played 60 minutes in the old days. They didn't have no offense and defense. They made you hurt when the game was over. There wasn't any offensive tackle and defensive tackle. You were a tackle, a guard, a center. Wasn't any flanker or end. All this tight end and all that stuff came and—everybody was tight.

---

[*] Comiskey Park, at 35th Street in South Chicago, was then home to the White Sox of baseball and the Cardinals of football.

Paul Stillwell: [Laughter] Have you ever reflected on why there were so many football players in the Golden 13?

Mr. Arbor: Everyone of us but Hair, Syl—[*]

Paul Stillwell: Cooper.[†]

Mr. Arbor: Cooper and Mummy. Those boys didn't have to [unclear] as Mummy.

Paul Stillwell: Was Big Barnes a football player?[‡]

Mr. Arbor: Big Barnes, yeah, in high school, didn't go to college. But the rest of us had to play football to make it. Syl, his daddy and mother were in the school system, I think. I know his daddy did.

    Alves's daddy was a preacher, so he had him a good thing going with all those kids.[§]

Paul Stillwell: Well, Hair got his scholarship sort of offhandedly. It was not related to his father. He met a man who had a connection with Loyola College, I believe, in New Orleans.[**]

Mr. Arbor: Yes, that's after he had gone to Bethune-Cookman in Florida. That's where he made a connection with the Loyola University thing in New Orleans, see. His first two years was in Florida. His junior and senior year was in New Orleans.

---

[*] James Edward Hair was a member of the Golden Thirteen; his oral history is in the Naval Institute collection. William Sylvester White was a member of the Golden Thirteen. His oral history is in the Naval Institute collection.

[†] George Clinton Cooper was a member of the Golden Thirteen. His oral history is in the Naval Institute collection.

[‡] Phillip George Barnes and Samuel Edward Barnes were both members of the Golden Thirteen. The oral history of Samuel Barnes is in the Naval Institute collection; Phillip Barnes died before he could be interviewed. Samuel Barnes was a football player and track man.

[§] Although he went all the way through officer training with the Golden Thirteen, A. Alves was not commissioned at the end of the training period.

[**] Hair actually attended Xavier University in New Orleans, not Loyola.

Mr. Jesse W. Arbor, Interview #2 (7/20/88) – Page 93

Paul Stillwell: And he was a basketball player.

Mr. Arbor: Oh, yes, yes. But that—

Paul Stillwell: Did you get the idea that the Navy was deliberately looking for football players for the group?

Mr. Arbor: No, no. See, when we went in, everybody from up until the selective service when everybody had to—they were drafting everybody. See, when we went in the Navy it was strictly all volunteers. We weren't drafted—none of us. The first 250,000-300,000 that went in were volunteers.*

Paul Stillwell: Well, in a sense. You volunteered because you were about to get drafted. [Laughter]

Mr. Arbor: I was forced to volunteer. [Laughter]

Paul Stillwell: That's right.

Mr. Arbor: But most all those boys had—give or take a few hundred or so—all those boys had high school or better. All of them. I don't know a one—

Paul Stillwell: Now, what group are we talking about?

Mr. Arbor: The first enlisted men in the Navy.

Paul Stillwell: Well, there were a lot who didn't. The ones that had the remedial reading program.

---

* Mr. Arbor may have been referring to enlistments by both black and white On 30 June 1945, at the height of World War II, The Navy had on active duty about 165,000 black enlisted personnel.

Mr. Arbor: They came in after the Selective Service Act.

Paul Stillwell: I see.

Mr. Arbor: But when it first opened up on June 1942—I forget the exact year now. Those who first went in, the first prerequisite was high school. That's where they started from. And most all of us who went in were in our 20s.

And we'd all been exposed to college, just about. All of us—every man in my boot camp had finished high school. And the ones in the next that I know—21, 22, and 23—companies 9, 21, 22, and 23—everybody'd finished high school. I forgot how many that had finished college.

So they had to have had some—and they were from all over the country, so they would have been exposed to football in high school or college. So they had to get the cream of the crop to as far as black students were concerned, because there wasn't anywhere else for them to go.

Same thing with the musicians, basketball players, entertainers, and all the guys like Duke Ellington, Cab Calloway, all those bands and things. Funny thing about it, they said they couldn't play music. [Laughter] They said they couldn't play band music. And Mr. George Parson—he was the chief judge in the northern district of Illinois, his district—had a master's degree in music. And they said he couldn't play music, couldn't play band music. He'd get it down there right now. And Lynn Bodden [phonetic], 87 years old—I was talking to him the other day. He set up all the bands, the colored bands—but they said he couldn't play band music. Oh, they had so many different stories. They couldn't do, couldn't do. They weren't given a chance. Anybody with a master's degree in music could read any kind of music. That's universal; music is. You don't have to speak the language; you can read the music.

And it used to intrigue me. It was like when Cab and Duke [unclear]—all those—Chick Webb [unclear]. If they were in town, he'd come up and play free.

The musicians, the leader of the band, couldn't introduce one of those bands. They had a chief musician—name was Oaks. So they added Peabody, who was a banjo picker with Lawrence Welk. He came in as a—I know he came in as a lieutenant commander, and in about three months' time they made a full commander of him just so he could introduce those bands and pick that banjo.

The Navy's come a long ways.

Paul Stillwell: So has the whole society.

Mr. Arbor: Umm-hmm. Oh, yeah. Umm-hmm.

Paul Stillwell: We didn't talk much about your service school time. Could you go into that, please, and the regimen there and what you learned?

Mr. Arbor: First we started off with semaphore, flashing lights. Then got into navigation. After that took place, we had chart courses, plotting, chart reading, sextants, azimuths, compasses. And theoretically, I was a good oarsman, I mean, steering. I never had my hand on a wheel till I went aboard that minesweeper. When I practiced so much mentally, I got good grades on that.

Paul Stillwell: Who were the instructors?

Mr. Arbor: We had a chief signalman. He was white. He'd had about 30 years in the Navy. We had a first class, no second class quartermaster. Quantz [phonetic] was his name—Harold Quantz. I forget what the old chief's name was, but they were damn good. We had a—I forget the guy who was teaching navigation. Can't remember his name. But we had [unclear], semaphore, and flashing light, signaling. And we had to learn some radio, on the radio signals. *The Bluejackets' Manual*—had to get up and plot your position from the star, so you knew you had to have a little knowledge in trig and algebra—thank God I had been exposed to both. I didn't know any of it, but I had been exposed to it. [Chuckle] Did so much with it I could do that. And my greatest pleasure was when I got out to sea. That's the most of the old things downstairs now, saw them in a footlocker the other day—some of my work that I did as a quartermaster third class.

Paul Stillwell: Did you find that very satisfying work?

Mr. Arbor: The heighth of my ambition was just to get up to be first class, set for first class. Never thought I'd ever be a chief, not to mention officer. All I wanted was to be up there, listen to the man on deck give the orders: "Right one quarter, left, steady as you go." So that's all I wanted. I could do that, instead of driving a ship. I'd have driven that thing 24 hours a day the first two or three days I was aboard—after I learned the pitch and rolling.

Paul Stillwell: You were probably among the first black rated quartermasters then.

Mr. Arbor: I don't know any other. I don't know any other ones, because we all started up at the same time. If there was any class that went out before me, because I was in the second quartermaster class. He said all those classes set up just for us—for "you people;" that was the word they used in those days.

Paul Stillwell: "You people."

Mr. Arbor: "You people." [Chuckle]

Paul Stillwell: Was that also at Robert Smalls?

Mr. Arbor: Umm-hmm. Yeah, where else? Everything was at Robert Smalls.

Paul Stillwell: How large was your service school class?

Mr. Arbor: Wasn't but 16. That's all there ever was.

Paul Stillwell: Were they training signalmen and quartermasters together?

Mr. Arbor: Well, see now, at the—I mean at the—

Paul Stillwell: Service school.

Mr. Arbor: Oh, service school was—I think it was about 18. About 30 to 40 in that class. I don't remember the exact number; it was 35 or 40. But the signalmen and quartermasters were in the same class.

Paul Stillwell: How did they determine which one you would be?

Mr. Arbor: The one with the eyes crossed, I guess, they sent him to signalman school. We all learned the same thing. We were taught the same thing: quartermaster and signalmen and radiomen.

I just wanted to mess with semaphores and flashing lights. I guess they made signalmen out of those. Ones who scored highest on charts, and diagrams, and maps, and things like that, I guess they made those quartermasters. That's the only reason I could differentiate between the two.

Paul Stillwell: How did you happen to get directed toward that particular rating?

Mr. Arbor: Aptitude test. Because I thought a quartermaster was like something in the Army—Army Corps. Because I had two brothers in the Army, quartermasters. At that time I thought that's what that was.

Paul Stillwell: They deal with supplies and things.

Mr. Arbor: That's all. They gave me a book with a wheel, compasses, sextants, tripods. I didn't know what the hell I was going to do with these two.

So after I got in that and I told my brothers what I was doing, "Oh, so you got it easy."

I said, "No, not like what you're thinking about. They don't issue anything." So it was an education for them to find out there's a difference between a quartermaster in the Army and a quartermaster in the Navy.

Paul Stillwell: Before the tape started, you were telling me how your group got headed from Great Lakes to the East Coast. I'd appreciate it if you could repeat that, please—about the draft and so forth.*

Mr. Arbor: Oh, I'm trying to recall where the—

Paul Stillwell: Well, there was one group that was, I guess, going to Boston—

Mr. Arbor: Oh, yes. Fun group—we all left as a unit and reported to the receiving station there at Boston. And then they called out, called our names, Brussard and Applewhite. No, they didn't send Brown. They sent us on pier one East Boston, and sent Brown, Collins, and Gaynor [phonetic] to Portsmouth, New Hampshire. They went up on a Navy base there. And Brown, I forget what boat—some small craft. And he ended up doing 20 years in the Navy, came out as a chief warrant officer.

Collins was a good writer. He ended up on the camp staff and was a reporter for the *Kansas City Star*. [Unclear] Gaynor ended up here as part of the police force. Brussard had bad health. I don't know what happened. He went back to Arizona. And I made a commission and the proudest feeling.

Collins was the one that taught me cadence in the head. And when I got my commission, he was on his way back to Kansas City to visit his mother. He heard about me, and he stopped out to the house. I went to the house. He'd been at the house. Mama took a liking to him. She thought he was too little to be in the Navy. He had red lips, like he had lipstick on him, he was so young and tender looking.

He walked up to me and he just started crying. He opened up a Coke and looked at me. He said, "Son, I'm proud of you. If it hadn't been for me, you wouldn't be here today." [Laughter]

Paul Stillwell: Maybe he was right.

---

* "Draft" is a term used to describe a group of service personnel traveling together to the same destination.

Mr. Arbor: He's right. We called him "Duck." He was so small. He was just asking, "What would have happened if I hadn't met you? Your mother wouldn't be as proud of you as she is if it hadn't been for me." [Laughter] He was the sweetest little thing I'd ever seen.

Paul Stillwell: Was your mother living in Illinois then?

Mr. Arbor: Yeah. Umm-hmm.

Paul Stillwell: What do you remember about your shipboard experience? What was the name of the vessel?

Mr. Arbor: AM-133, the *Hawk*.[*]

Paul Stillwell: And what was the name of that one that Baugh went to?[†]

Mr. Arbor: *Truant*.

Paul Stillwell: How large a ship was it?

Mr. Arbor: Well, the *Truant* was Henry Ford's personal yacht converted. That was a pretty good—it was seaworthy. Mine was seaworthy too but not as big as Baugh's. Mine was like a Jeep parked beside a Cadillac, alongside a large ship.

Paul Stillwell: Do you remember approximately how big she was?

Mr. Arbor: No, I don't.

---

[*] USS *Hawk* (AM-133) was acquired by the Navy on 1 January 1942 and converted from a steel-hulled fishing trawler to a minesweeper. She was commissioned 23 May 1942. She was 147 feet long, 26 feet in the beam, had a maximum draft of 13 feet, and displaced 540 tons. Her top speed was 11.5 knots.
[†] Dalton Louis Baugh was a member of the Golden Thirteen. He died before he could be interviewed by the Naval Institute's oral history program.

Paul Stillwell: How large a crew did you have?

Mr. Arbor: We had 26. They must have had twice as many on that. That fellow was seaworthy. You could take off and go anywhere.

Paul Stillwell: How many officers were there in the *Hawk*?

Mr. Arbor: Three.

Paul Stillwell: Were they the only whites?

Mr. Arbor: Umm-hmm. No, we had a chief; we had a white first class boatswain. A white lieutenant was skipper. Jaygee was XO. Had an ensign who was first lieutenant. Three white officers.

Paul Stillwell: How well did the crew get along with each other?

Mr. Arbor: Oh, fine, fine. I never was on a ship or anything—there wasn't that I could say that wherever I went anything went wrong. Looked like I was just lucky. They got the instructions just like I did from the Navy: whether you liked it or not, you obeyed your commands. And there wasn't too many dummies in that man's Navy that I know of in our group, just to be frank with you. But they saw to that on the front side coming in. They never started having any trouble until they started drafting. Then, of course, the Army started complaining. But before they started universal draft, all the smart blacks were going into the Navy. Because they hadn't started in the Marine Corps then. And then they broke down and started—a number so many X, you know. X number go to the Navy, X number, and Army, and Marines. And I don't think they started certain drafting [unclear]. I think it was still voluntary up until—then they started getting the older type men, 35-30—just this side. They just wouldn't wait until they made 37; it was 18 to 37. Because I remember in my outfit they sent a man up to Boston. I came back on a ship, they sent a man and his son there in the same draft. Old man was 38—they got him before he was 37. [Chuckle] His son volunteered; his mama signed him in. They separated and they ended up—and the boy was—of course, they went along just like they didn't know each other. I forget what was his last name.

Paul Stillwell: Why would they do that?

Mr. Arbor: I don't know, because after the Sullivan brothers got killed on that ship, they swore they wouldn't have another family together.* It could have been just a slipup, of course—where the father, there was his son, they were playing poker up at the barracks one night. And his son and some old boys got to cursing down there, and playing the [unclear] with each other. And the [unclear] jumped up. He couldn't stand it no longer. Went down and talked about the way he did to his mother out in the street that night. The old man was sitting there. He jumped out and grabbed the boy's arm. He said, "I can't hear if that's my son. He's talking about my wife."

I said, "That's all right. You can't whip him in the Navy." I said, "He's as big a man as you are." So he [unclear section]. Everybody found out it was father and son. He had to laugh. I said, "That ain't going to stop." I said, "You used to talk like that. You cursed, talking about your sister and boots and all that kind of stuff. [Unclear] when you were his age." I said, "You just [unclear]."

We laughed about that a long time. He said, "But he's talking about my wife now. That's his mother."

Paul Stillwell: These were guys in the *Hawk*?

Mr. Arbor: No, that was in the barracks getting ready to be assigned to a ship.

Paul Stillwell: I see.

---

* Five brothers from the Sullivan family of Waterloo, Iowa, were lost when the light cruiser *Juneau* (CL-52) was sunk off Guadalcanal on 13 November 1942.

Mr. Arbor: No, they never did make it to some ship. See, we'd go out in the morning and come back in at night. We had access up to a rec hall up in the barracks, but we didn't have one of them until we had—until about 11:00 o'clock and we'd go back and go aboard ship and go to sleep. So we'd always go back up to the barracks there off the pier there and play cards and shoot pool. Now that was a nice place. I guess they had about 50-50, white and black up there in rooms. They had a darn good cook there, and they let us eat up there. We had good food on the ship. But [unclear] get more and taste better than what—and a great big pool hall, pool tables, and ping-pong games. It was nice up there. USO was there from time to time in those days.* So those boys who didn't know how to get down to the city of Boston, it didn't make any difference. It didn't bother me because I'd been running in and out there. I'd been there about a year almost.

Paul Stillwell: It sounds as if the men got along quite harmoniously.

Mr. Arbor: Oh, yeah. Yeah. I never saw one incident of any kind that you could consider as racial. Even back there. Of course, there was that Marine on the gate hated me because I didn't stand guard duty. [Chuckle] You wouldn't consider that as a racial incident. He was nice and quiet when I was on that gate, and I ran my big mouth, "What were you doing on there? Don't you have nowhere to go?" I could rag him in those days.

Paul Stillwell: I think you still have some of those qualities today.

Mr. Arbor: [Laughter]

Paul Stillwell: Why do you think that the people got along so well together?

Mr. Arbor: Oh, number one, it was all when you came in, and they start telling you the rules and regs of the Navy, that each one of us was dependent on the other. "Now, this is your family until you are out of the Navy." And then, those of us who had been out in the

---

* USO – United Services Organization is a group of U.S. civilians who put on entertainment programs for service personnel and provide hospitality for them in many parts of the world.

world and to school and been exposed to life could very easily set an example for those little 17-18-year-old kids and kind of guide them through.

Because now, to tell the truth, everybody was given the same uniform; everybody was lined up to go to the chow hall. "Now, it's up to you—now, if you can't get along with me, that's your fault. You've got to stay here. You can't jump over in the harbor. I've got to get along with you, so we might as well start off like we're [unclear]. Because you can't jump overboard. Where are you going if you jump overboard? Instead of AWOL, you've got to come back some day."* And they had to set up divisions and things like that. If something goes wrong, they go along with the chain of command. They do that so that no matter how mad you are before you get up to the top, the old man, somebody will have cooled you off. I believe that's why it's set up what's desired. You just can't start in and jump up on the bridge and tell the old man. You have to go through step by step. And in that time you get to somebody who'll cool you off, let you know who's wrong, or the other fellow was wrong, have him come down, and you all get together.

I never did encounter, either as an officer or as an enlisted man, any occasion where I saw it necessary that I should go to anybody, or have anybody reprimand me for, you know, improper conduct. It was just part of my—I never did do it in civilian life. And I took that on in the Navy with me. And if I saw anybody—the best thing to do is keep them on time and clean; everything else will take care of itself.

Paul Stillwell: Those are two big things in the Navy.

Mr. Arbor: See, especially everybody's going to have a buddy—or one or two. If we went out liberty together, I'd say, "If you're going to get your head tight tonight, I'm not. We've got to be back there by 12:00 o'clock or 1:00 o'clock, somebody's got to go, you're not going to be late. Whatever you're doing, you can finish it before time for that train going back to East Boston. Never be late and stay clean."

Paul Stillwell: And do what you're told is the third one.

---

* AWOL—absent without leave. The Navy equivalent for this term is UA—unauthorized absence.

Mr. Arbor: That's the first one.

Paul Stillwell: That's right. That's the first one.

Mr. Arbor: That is the very first, and all those youngsters wanted to follow me, because they knew I would be on time. If it got into anything in the city, I'd be in it. And I knew not to fight. "What do you want to fight for? If I whip you, I can't eat you; I can't take you home with me. You can call me a coward if you want; I'm going to talk my way out of it and them be [unclear]." And no buddy of mine that we went on liberty, and God knows there were occasions where there would have been plenty. "I'll just stand here a few minutes. I'll either fail or pass, or we leave." If we were in a bar or something like that and I smelled a rat, I'd say, "Something is going to jump you. Let's get out of here. Somebody might throw a chair and hit me upside the head."

Paul Stillwell: How were you treated by civilians?

Mr. Arbor: Oh, during the war anywhere you went, everybody loved you. Now, as long as it wasn't the city of Chicago, you didn't have to pay carfare, bus fare, train fare, nothing.

Paul Stillwell: Did civilians buy drinks for you?

Mr. Arbor: Oh, yeah. The longest bar in the world at that time was supposed to be down on 63rd Street. You'd go in there, a five- or six-piece band. There were old men. There might be 150-200 or more people. They had four or five old men, daddies and granddaddies. And one sailor or soldier come in there, boy, the whiskeys came sliding down the bar.

Paul Stillwell: They weren't entirely unselfish in those gestures.

Mr. Arbor: They had the right approach. They had the right [unclear]

Paul Stillwell: Did you have a chance to exercise some leadership and responsibility as a petty officer in the *Hawk*?

Mr. Arbor: Only in rank. See, because it's the same thing as a family in one of those small ships. Everybody was everybody else's concern. Even the captain didn't have too much of a leadership role, because the thing was so uniquely set up. They'd post that watch list, and everybody saw that that next man was going to be up out of that bunk, ready and at his post and on his watch.

Everybody was too glad to be aboard, it looked like, because we—I had the single ambition when I left Robert Smalls—to go aboard ship.

Paul Stillwell: Why do you say that?

Mr. Arbor: Because going aboard ship topside and not going as a mess attendant.

Paul Stillwell: A lot of pride.

Mr. Arbor: They had a lot of pride. They wanted to go to sea as a sailor, not as a cook or steward. And that's all what I was ducking. That's all any of us were ducking.

Paul Stillwell: How patriotic would you say were the black sailors of that era?

Mr. Arbor: They'd give their right arm or leg or life—as long as they thought that skipper was fair. And everyone I've ever worked under, if he wasn't, he had a damn good way of faking it.

So that's about a routine. I know that I was around. I'd never been into squabbling or grumbling until I got overseas. And that bunch that they brought in—that little bunch of draftees that they ran through boot camp for about eight or ten weeks and sent to Port Chicago and Port Hueneme, California.* Unloading that ammo didn't tell them what they were doing and hadn't instructed and killed I don't know how many of them. All that was left, they put them all in a group and sent them—they should have dispersed those kids. Sent them down to different islands, two or three islands in the Pacific and start punishing them. Why punish them? They were out playing volleyball or something. They didn't know anything about ammo. Those young kids, that if they'd had the right talent, they would have been in high school had they been at home. You take them out to the [unclear] streets and teach them left, right, left, right for about six weeks. And then put them out there, load them with forklifts and jeeps and trucks and them little devils learn how to drive. Shoot, they didn't know what they were doing.

That's one thing that irks you. The Navy sure kept quiet.

Paul Stillwell: You're right.

Mr. Arbor: Up until this day, we've run across quite a few of them sometime. Two or three of them around here are still bitter. And there's that Navy convention be here next week. Quite a few of them in that, and they're still bitter: "If they had just told us and taught us how—[unclear]. And then they blamed us. We didn't know—crates were all we knew. And they had us rushing to see which one section would do more. That's the part that hurts."

Now you run across somebody like these [unclear]. He's frightened. He's afraid of everybody. And you see them put him on one of those ships, and you can toss, and bob, and bob, and bob—only thing on it is God-forsaken atolls or something out there in the Pacific. Then he starts in about his old slavery-type experiences he's heard. He said, "They brought me over in a ship, and they take me out of here on water." And all that.

I said, "What consideration are you giving those kids?" You take them up and meet with a psychiatrist or psychologist—that's where they should have gone.

---

* On the night of 17 July 1944, 320 individuals, 202 of whom were black ammunition handlers, were killed when two merchant ships, the *Quinalt Victory* and the *E. A. Bryan*, exploded while being loaded with munitions at Port Chicago, California, about 40 miles northeast of San Francisco. A number of the ammunition handlers were subsequently court-martialed because of their reluctance to go back to dangerous work. See Robert L. Allen, *The Port Chicago Mutiny* (New York: Warner Books, Inc., 1989).

Paul Stillwell: How do you explain that sense of patriotism in view of the fact that the nation as a whole was so unfair in its treatment of blacks?

Mr. Arbor: You know, the setting was unique—the training—and we all went through it, into it. But, more or less, all inherited, God-given inheritance. Always do your best, and the best will return some day, somehow. That was part of my old man's philosophy. Never do anything to anyone that you don't want them to do unto you first. Always do your best, and the best will come back to you. Give to the world the best you have, and the best will come back to you. That permeates all of our lives to a certain degree, some more or less.

I've always said in order to accomplish anything, first set your goals. The Lord told it. It's going to be very, very few occasions—of course, nothing will always run smooth—it's like a ship, the roll of the waves. This is a hard-hearted man, or hard-hearted nation for any individual. To keep going, it's almost [unclear] when it's not easy. It might take years, months, maybe hundreds of years. But, finally, if there is any justice in this world at all, and we all believe in a true God. If I can't lie prostrate on my knees, and begging the good Lord all the time and working, doing what I'm told, and keep the whip off my back, I just don't exist. In the Navy I must say it was far ahead of the social life of the country from which we all came. See, all the services are just a microcosm of everyday life. The Navy was a little bit further. They were a little bit more tolerant and understanding than the other branches. Even today I think so. Everything isn't peaches and cream out here on Ridgeland.* But life is what you make it. And I've made a pretty damn good life for myself and my family. Three kids, one with a master's; he's 12-year tenured. The baby girl has left; she's over at Osco. Son [unclear] 12 years. I'm the sorriest one in the group.

Paul Stillwell: I doubt that.

Mr. Arbor: Wife's a principal. She's getting ready to retire after 30 years. So how can I say life's been cruel to me? But I had to work at it. I tell any individual, "You should

---

* The interview took place in Arbor's home on South Ridgeland Avenue in Chicago.

meet somebody continually high all their lives, I'll show you somebody hasn't put 100% effort in anything." We're all going to fail at something, but somewhere after 35-40 or 40 years—your 40th birthday, you should have in mind just about the direction you want to go. If you haven't made up your mind by that time, you're feebleminded.

That's one of the things I'm teaching my son now. He's 38 and he wants to go back to school.

I said, "Son, you can't be a professional student. You know your old man was 35 years old when you were born." [Chuckle] I said, "I can't sponsor you anymore." I said, "I'm retired now." I said, "You can do whatever you want to do." [Unclear] I said, "But by this time in life, you should have a pretty good idea the direction you want to take in life." I said, "When you get over there where you think you want to go, it's not what you think it is. There's always a struggle. Life is a struggle. [Unclear] it's a struggle if you accomplish anything. Anything one does, if it's hard work, if you make it hard work. If you think it's hard, it's hard. If I had to go back over it again, I'd go right back over the same road, same way—same road but not the same way.

Paul Stillwell: Well, I'm sure all of us could find ways to do it better because we know more now.

Mr. Arbor: Yes, that's 20/20 hindsight.

Paul Stillwell: What are some of the operations you remember from serving in the *Hawk*? What sorts of things did the ship do?

Mr. Arbor: We would leave about, 0530 or 0600 in the morning. We'd sweep mines out past the gate along the degaussing lines and pick up a tail about a block behind the ship.* The thing I never could figure out was that magnetic line back there. If you look at me, we should have had that damn thing front. [Laughter] Be a long time before I could figure out that if I was going to blow up a mine back here and we'd—sometimes the

---

* Degaussing is the practice of wrapping electrical cables around the hull of a ship to reduce its magnetic tendencies. Ships run a degaussing range to check the effectiveness of the equipment.

degaussing systems were rigged up the way the ship, and the magnetic tail would draw it back there. We'd sweep out until about 1:30 or 2:00 o'clock in the afternoon. Then we'd turn around and come back in, sweep for all the ships coming in. Four or five of them were out there. So we had the whole to breadth to sweep to come in the gates that had been blocked with a lot of mines so nobody could come in. Then they'd pull that gate open. That was the daily routine. Now, the one Baugh was on, they went out a little further. They didn't come back in at night. That's the one we all wanted to get on and get out there. I got on one of that had nothing, had no lodging on board. That's one I was supposed to go and they called me back. I was going to give it a try on that. But—

Paul Stillwell: How long did you serve in the *Hawk*?

Mr. Arbor: Six months.

Paul Stillwell: When was that—'43, early '43?

Mr. Arbor: January to sometime up in July.

Paul Stillwell: And then from there to the *Guinevere*?

Mr. Arbor: No, from there back to Harvard University School of Navigation. And then I came off that. And then I made second class in the *Guinevere*.*

Paul Stillwell: What did you learn at Harvard that qualified you for second class?

Mr. Arbor: Advanced navigation. That's what I learned all that.

Paul Stillwell: Celestial?

---

* USS *Guinevere* (IX-67) was an auxiliary schooner built in 1921 and acquired by the Navy on 24 March 1942. She was commissioned 16 June 1942. She was 195 feet long, 32 feet in the beam, had a draft of 15 feet, and displaced 503 tons. After a brief shakedown she performed harbor patrol duties at Boston and escorted newly formed convoys out to sea.

Mr. Arbor: Umm-hmm. And weather charts, things like that. Cloud formation, prediction of rain possible.

[Telephone interruption]

Paul Stillwell: Did you have a larger crew in the second ship?

Mr. Arbor: Oh, yeah. We had—definitely. We had about 40-50 or more.

Paul Stillwell: Was it essentially the same type of operation?

Mr. Arbor: Yeah, but now we had one machine gun forward and one aft. I forget now, but they had a first class gunner's mate on that thing. And we had an antiaircraft battery on the front and aft. That was hooked up pretty good. We were wired up for battles.

Paul Stillwell: Could you go out farther in that one?

Mr. Arbor: Oh, yeah, umm-hmm. That was strictly a seaworthy one. They would sweep and patrol. We were strictly a sweeper. That's the one—that's what I was jealous about, as big as a light cruiser. Like one of those little DEs, I would say.

Paul Stillwell: Umm-hmm. Did your crew have the same sense of family that you'd known in the smaller ship?

Mr. Arbor: Always, it looked like, only the family was larger. And they had about a 60-40, about a 60% white crew on that one. They had the first class gunner's mate; I don't know how the rates were in the engine room. I think they had a chief—I could be wrong on that, but I do know that they had a first class boatswain, had a first class fireman down there too. When they'd come up to eat, I'd see them. And a chief boatswain on that ship. So that'd be pretty good size to have a chief anything.

Paul Stillwell: Right. Were there instances in which white men were working for black men?

Mr. Arbor: The way the watches ran, I don't know if they were working for them, but they were working side by side. Because now you work in the Navy according to your Navy rate or rank.

Paul Stillwell: Right.

Mr. Arbor: Well, we just got there. We couldn't have had any rate or rank.

Paul Stillwell: Well, you were a second class.

Mr. Arbor: Well, now, see, under me there was a third class, which happened to be black. But there wasn't no first class quartermaster on there, but there was a first class signalman. He was white.

Paul Stillwell: Did you and he get along well?

Mr. Arbor: Oh, fine. I get along with him [unclear]. I can get along with anyone, anywhere. Even when times were rough, I got along. Because I was always good to judge personalities. I could tell in, oh, less than three minutes—from the time we shake hands and say, "Good morning," or "Hello," whether we were going to hit it off or have anything in common. Then I'd absent myself quickly. No use sticking around [unclear]. You don't have time to hand-raise anybody or housebreak them, [chuckle] or those things. I always will believe that the Navy had some system in judging personnel, because I know whenever I go aboard some of these ships now, which is quite frequent, the first thing I do, I get down. An officer will guide me all over the ship. I get down with the enlisted men, and some of them will break down and they tell me what's going on.

"I don't know, He scratched my back or he did this."

I said, "Chances are I can help you, and chances are I can't help you. I can't make any promises, but I can get further than you can. Nothing petty now." You say nothing petty, you cut out one-half of the complaints. Because all of us could gripe about something. But now that whole day is passed when he has to be white, or he has to be black to be relegated to this, or elevated thus and so; it took time. But for the grace of God, what would happen if the shoe was on the other foot? That's the way you look at life. This is a fact of race, and nothing remains constant but change.

Paul Stillwell: Did white men and black men go on liberty together from those ships?

Mr. Arbor: Very seldom. Very seldom. Now I just—the watch was set up that way. Are they going with first class or second? There were no first class or chiefs and on down to go on liberty with. So you stayed with people of—surrounded by that you're familiar with. The chief didn't go with admirals or captains. First class didn't run with the chiefs. And after I got to be an officer, they always had the senior officer sitting over behind there with all those scrambled eggs on their hats.* And then the extra wardroom, the little ensigns didn't go in there. Jaygees, full lieutenants, captains, and on up had their own. Now, commanders and lieutenant commanders, they've got to hobnob lightly together. But the higher up on that rank you went, you stayed in your own group. That's the class they run in.

So there was no such thing as enlisted men going together on leave because they were not aiming first class anything. And as soon as they got first class, I mean second class the whole system had begin to change then, because it took about four or five years until you got up to first class, even in wartime, three good years. By that time you formulate your own habits and patterns. Because when you get in town, everything went—you don't legislate morale nor mores. That's a natural phenomenon. And I never did believe in polishing apples or polishing over something to make it look so. If it was not the real McCoy, don't bring it to me, because I don't have sense enough to polish apples. [Chuckle]

---

* "Scrambled eggs" is slang for the gold-colored decorations on the visor of a senior naval officer's cap.

Mr. Jesse W. Arbor, Interview #2 (7/20/88) – Page 113

Paul Stillwell: Well, we all do some of that, I'm sure.

Mr. Arbor: Oh, [unclear] they say, but what I'm talking about is to go overboard to say everything is peaches and cream when I know it's not. But circumstances have been of such that is the way life was set up. Now I did more socializing as an officer than I did as an enlisted man, because I was the only one. Everywhere I went up until I got over to Guam, the chaplain came over there. No, Lear was a warrant officer.* So it was intriguing that most of them wanted to talk to me to see why I was born, where, what for. Did I cry when I was a baby? So it never occurred to me that it was so depressing to be on—to contact me. Of course, I'd been on my own all my life—waiter, bellboy, receiving clerk, and a Pullman porter.

Paul Stillwell: Well, you had really been forced to accommodate to the white society.

Mr. Arbor: Umm-hmm. And at the time nobody worked for the Pullman Company but the cream of the crop. I followed—I had the pleasure of working with Helen Hayes one entire summer. [Unclear]—I got started at Cincinnati, all the towns, two-night stands all the way down to Louisville, Nashville, New Orleans, Jacksonville, back up to Atlanta. Had only cars [unclear] time.

And had one group took all the way from here to Seattle on excursion. I mean, they had the entire train, see. Back in those days, I've been all over with all the big shots. So being around people of different races, attitudes, financial status was nothing new to me.

Paul Stillwell: I think that there was a difference, though, that those people on the trains probably didn't think of you as an individual. They thought of you as somebody who provided a service.

Mr. Arbor: Could be.

---

* Charles Byrd Lear was a member of the Golden Thirteen. He died shortly after World War II.

Paul Stillwell: It was different when you were in the Navy. They had to recognize you as an individual.

Mr. Arbor: Some did. Now, the only real incident, and it didn't occur to me that ordinarily I would have busted a gut—was the night I got to Guam. There was no schedule. Flying military flights when you get there, you're on time. But the little sailor that picked me up at the airfield didn't know where I was supposed to go. He didn't know where the BOQ was.* BOQ was mostly tents. [Unclear] So he said, "Here's where the officers live here." So I went in there, and there was a vacant bed. Something like the way they install things in hospitals.

So I went in there. He said, "Now, I got orders to be back here and pick you up at 0630, take you down, and show you where you get your chow."

I said, "Okay, sailor." [Unclear]

So I went on in, and there was no use taking a bath because there was no water there. So next morning somebody said, "Bob, Bob!"

So I didn't say anything—I didn't know whether there's some new stalls on that side or this side. So this guy came up. He was a commander. He said, "Where is Bob?"

I said, "I don't know Bob. I just came in here about one o'clock last night, I guess. I don't even know what time it is."

He said, "You mean to tell me you slept here all night?"

I said, "Not all night, but since I got here."

He said, "Well, goddamn! You mean to tell me I staying on a [unclear] with one of you fellows all night? I'll be damned."

I said, "What's your name?"

He didn't tell me. So I went up to report to the island commander. I told them what had happened.

"Wait just a minute. He'll be here in a few minutes. He's got to leave this island, and he said he doesn't want to."

I said, "This is going to hurry him up."

---

* BOQ – bachelor officers' quarters.

Paul Stillwell: [Laughter]

Mr. Arbor: He walked in and looked at me. "You up here?"

I said, "What are you talking about?" I was beginning to get mad now. At that time, everybody was issued a .45. I had mine on; he had his on. Now that he was all a force of dignity and self-restraint, I wanted to keep him a little bit cool, you see. And this island commander was looking green. He said, "There's your driver there. He's going to take you over to your command."

Paul Stillwell: He said this to you?

Mr. Arbor: Umm-hmm. General Larson was his name.

He said, "This sailor's going to take you up to your command." And he shook my hand and walked me to the aisle. He said, "You can sit down here."

I'd sure like to know what he said to him. I haven't seen him since. That's the only incident that you might say was unpleasant that I ran into. And I didn't run into that; he ran into me.

And the funniest one I had was when I was at Pearl Harbor. There were about 35-40 officers in their barracks there. And Lear and I were the only two blacks. The skipper, a commander, was from New Orleans. He wanted for us to play poker with him every night, he and some officer. It was a 25- or 50-cent poker game, just mostly to pass the time away. Lear didn't play poker with us, so he would play the other fun and games around there. Hell, I was good in draw poker or stud poker as anybody. Every night after chow, the captain came in, "Mr. Arbor, we're going to have a little poker game up here in the wardroom. If you would like to join us." Two or three nights I did refuse. Just got there, and I wanted to see who was who.

So after I was there about three or four weeks, I met a guy named Archibald Douglas, who used to be a radio announcer. He came in as a jaygee. He said, "Say, Arbor, why don't you come on down and join us? The captain really thinks you're scared to play poker." Doug said, "Let's go down."

So I went on down and, hat up, seven-card game. Well, you don't, draw; you don't need too many men in there. Only 52 cards in a deck. How are you going to play poker with eight, or nine, or ten players? [Laughter] You only get two cards apiece.

So I said, "Otherwise, if we're going to play in your game, we have to play by your rules." So they had everything wild, and there was money. Jokers wild and one-eyed jacks and all that, everything wild. So I sat down, and every time I'd catch a hand, it would be just a [unclear]. Sometimes I would turn it in and throw it away. Just to keep them even.

Paul Stillwell: Why did you throw it away?

Mr. Arbor: I don't know. This was my first game, see. So we went all—so this went on, I guess, four or five months. And I never will forget, about the month before I left there for Guam, I quit playing poker. We were playing straight five-card stud.

"Well, Mr. Arbor, we're playing your game now."

"I know I can beat you at this one." Set them up.

Every time I'd pick up my hand—sometime I—I said, "Well, Captain, I'm not going to take your money now because I'm not married and you are. You need your money." I was razzing him, going to beat him out of $400 or $500.

He said, "Don't leave them lying down. Deal them up."

I said, "You can't raise but three times." I said, "Because if you come off this game, you can turn me around. You got some of these other light players around." Just ran my mouth.

He dealt me up. He said, "Now, Mr. Arbor, you're just lucky."

So I never would deal, because I didn't want them to think that I was a fake. But I had a good memory and if you're going play poker, you got to remember every card going around, and bet on that you haven't got the hole card. I was young in those days. So this night I know I'm going to leave tomorrow [unclear]. I led [unclear]

Paul Stillwell: You dealt?

Mr. Arbor: I dealt. So I never will forget. I said, "Now I better let the captain deal, because it's walking day. So he dealt himself a full house—kings over ten. He dealt me three treys to start out with—one, two, three. He got two pair on the [unclear]. I got two pair, but they're all threes. [Chuckle] He bet [unclear]. I raised him. All around the table, wouldn't was nobody get out of the game because it's got a quarter limit. He raised—everybody can raise it three times. Somebody at the table [unclear] high. So it got back to me, and I raised. Every time it'd get to me, I'd bump it. So every time it'd get to him, he got a full house. And I didn't have nothing but treys. And here come the fifth card. I had a pair of treys; he got a pair of kings. He gives me an ace; he gets an ace. No, he—ten, that's what it is, ten. That gave him tens, and I got four treys. We got to betting up there and got pretty good. So I said, "Captain, since I'm going to leave the island and I don't need no money, I'm going to raise you the last time. If you bump me again, I'm going to have to pull the cover off this game."

So the exec says, "No," he says, "I ain't got but a little more money here so this is—rules of the game, when you lose all your money, you lose your seat to somebody else. That's all you can do, is sit down. You can't go back to your room and get some more money. If you lose all your money and won't nobody let you have any, you got to give it to someplace else."

So he called, "Well, Mr. Arbor, I say," he says, "I got a full house. I got kings over."

He started reaching for the money, I said, "Wait a minute."

He says, "What have you got?"

"I got two pair, Captain, but they're all treys."

Paul Stillwell: [Laughter]

Mr. Arbor: So he said, "I knew there was a goddamn nigger in the wood pile somewhere." [Laughter]*

I sat right there and listened like I hadn't heard anything.

---

* Mr. Arbor told a condensed version of this episode in his first interview. The two versions differ, particularly in his account of which cards he had.

So everybody left at 11:00 o'clock. We had to quit at 11:30 because curfew was on {unclear]. So I [unclear] turned the room and left and everybody was just laughing.

After a while somebody knocked on the door. He had a fifth of whiskey or something in his hand. He said [Arbor imitated a southern accent], "Mr. Arbor, I came by here to apologize."

"For what, Captain," I said. "Four treys beat a full house anytime."

He said, "That ain't what I come down here for."

"You want to borrow something, Captain?"

"No," he said, "Did you honestly hear what I said at the table up there?"

"I heard you say you have a full house."

He said, "That's all you heard?"

I said, "That's all I heard." I said, "I got the money. Some of the officers said I didn't have—I showed them my hand.

He shook my hand and said, "I used an expression that I make when I'm around all white folks. You didn't hear?"

I said, "No, Captain. You are an officer and a gentleman." [Laughter]

Paul Stillwell: You were lying.

Mr. Arbor: I was lying, but it was fun—it was fun. Now, where would I go to get hot about? I'd used the expression myself.

Paul Stillwell: Oh, really? [Laughter] What was this man's name? Do you remember?

Mr. Arbor: Grady Avant.* Never will forget him.

One of the little [unclear]. They set me up there because he was—he was a World War I Army officer. He switched over from Army to Navy because "I'm from the South, and I understand all the colored people." And right out there, "Well, you know, Mr. Arbor, I was brought up with colored folks and [unclear]. Now I see your side."

---

* Lieutenant Commander Grady Avant, USNR.

I said, "Captain, if you were brought up with colored folks, colored folks were brought up with you. Now, you can't be brought up, one on one side and one—we were brought up together. I said, "Well . . ."

He says, "I was a little closer than most folks."

I said, "You don't have to go into all that, you don't have to tell me that you had a white mammy that you sucked on."

"Yeah."

I said, "Now, is it necessary that I should go through all that? I should have been your black mammy." I didn't sit [unclear]. He got off that. I've just been that crazy all my life. I said, "I'm not out here to be patronized, or eulogized, or pitied. I came out here to do a job for the Navy, just like you." [Unclear] ever come up on that old "I love colored folks. I was brought up with them."

Paul Stillwell: What was his point in saying all that?

Mr. Arbor: I never could figure it out. There was no occasion for that to arise. But every occasion—you can find any one of those officers—and, in civilian life—want to show you how much he loves black people by telling how he came up with them.

Paul Stillwell: Was Armstrong along those lines?

Mr. Arbor: Oh, he was the epitome of such. He knew every hair, ever tooth in any black man's head: "You're colored people." Oh, I couldn't stand that man at all.

Paul Stillwell: Was he condescending?

Mr. Arbor: Very much so. I just couldn't stand the man. I never saw him that much.

Paul Stillwell: How much contact did you have with him?

Mr. Arbor: The only contact I had with him personally was when he handed me—when he gave me that commission. "How did you get here?" Didn't say, "Congratulations, good morning, get out and [unclear]."

Paul Stillwell: It's interesting. I talked to Mr. Williams this morning, and he liked Armstrong.

Mr. Arbor: Oh, Reggie Goodwin and Mummy had no reason to—they were what you called the "Big House Boys."* They knew everything that Armstrong knew and more. They're well educated, both of them. And they were working right in their field of education. See when the dummies started coming through, that gave them a cause for Mummy to set up a remedial school, he and Goody. The Navy did. Right up their alleys. But the rest of us, we weren't there trying to educate anybody. We were trying to get along and get out. Now, what made Reggie so hot, when Armstrong got shipped out, they shipped him out. Sent him to Eniwetok. And he was bitter until the day he died about that.

Paul Stillwell: Well, Armstrong was sort of his patron then.

Mr. Arbor: Patron saint.

Paul Stillwell: How often did Armstrong talk to your group or have dealings with them?

Mr. Arbor: The only time I ever saw that man at a—I mean, other than going across—they had a regimental room drill before they had that whole regiment, 18th Regiment, graduated at the same time. And I saw him up on the stage and talking about "you people." And I disliked him calling us "you sailors, you fine sailormen." And he had little Hathcock—he had a master's degree in music too. He was over in the music department. Shucks, got that from Morris Brown University.

---

* Reginald Ernest Goodwin was a member of the Golden Thirteen. He died before he could be interviewed by the Naval Institute's oral history program.

Armstrong wrote a song just for the 18th Regiment. [Arbor singing], "They look like men, they act like men; I think they will be great men of war." I wouldn't sing it. I sang "Anchors Aweigh" or something like that, yes. He went for, "They look like men; they act like men; I think they will make great men of war." Isn't that condescending?

Paul Stillwell: Yes.

Mr. Arbor: And very few of the guys would sing it. They tell you to stand up; you stand up. We had to stand up. You can't make us sing. Give us "Attention!" Everybody would come to attention. That's Navy. But we don't have to sing. [Laughter]

Paul Stillwell: Hathcock was on that list of men you sent me who were considered officer candidates. Why didn't he go through the training with you?

Mr. Arbor: I don't know. I don't know. I never saw Hathcock, and some kind of chief storekeeper was on there. I don't know why he didn't make it. Some kind of chief storekeeper.

Paul Stillwell: Here's the list.

Mr. Arbor: Cooper, Barnes, Baugh, Williams, Sublett, Nelson, Pinkney, Martin, Goodwin, Hathcock, Barnes (Sam), White, Reagan (John), Lear, Alves, Powell, [unclear]. Where did—what happened to him?

Paul Stillwell: Did you see him at all?

Mr. Arbor: Never saw him. I don't know whether he was another Pinkney or what.[*] They must have discovered him before he got there. I never found out what happened to

---

[*]. Although he went all the way through officer training with the Golden Thirteen, J. B. Pinkney was not commissioned at the end of the training period.

Baugh. And up until I left the Navy, I never saw the name Powell show up anywhere. So I wonder what happened to Chief Powell."

Paul Stillwell: One of the other fascinating things about this list is that Hair's name is misspelled.* No, Hair's not even on this list. He was on another list.

Mr. Arbor: Hair's name is not misspelled. Hair is misspelling his name now.

Paul Stillwell: [Laughter] No, Hair was on the list that's in Nelson's book, but he's not on this list from the Assistant Chief of Naval Personnel.

Mr. Arbor: It's not?

Paul Stillwell: Well, I don't see it.

Mr. Arbor: Cooper, Barnes, Baugh, Nelson, Hathcock.

Paul Stillwell: Maybe Hair took the place of one of those other two.

Mr. Arbor: Another name's not on here. Ain't no Arbor on there.

Paul Stillwell: [Laughter] That's right too. Well, I guess maybe you two bumped those others.

Mr. Arbor: Now I've got another list where all of us are on, including those names.

Paul Stillwell: I think that's the list in Nelson's book.†

---

* As Hair explained in his own oral history, at the time he was undergoing officer training, he was temporarily spelling his last name as H-A-R-E, and that was the spelling used on his official Navy records.
† Ensign Dennis Denmark Nelson II, USNR. He eventually retired from the Navy as a lieutenant commander. He died in 1979 before he could be interviewed as part of the Naval Institute's oral history program. Nelson's master's thesis was published by the Navy Department in 1948 and later came out as a book, *The Integration of the Negro into the U.S. Navy* (New York: Farrar, Strauss and Young, 1951).

Mr. Arbor: Umm-hmm. I look at this list all the way down; I still don't see a Powell.

Paul Stillwell: Well, he wasn't commissioned apparently. These are the ones that became officers.

Mr. Arbor: Oh, yeah, yeah. Here. Now Hair—this is the way he's listed. Went to college on that name. Hair got married under that name and went into the Navy under that name, H-A-I-R, is the name he got after he got out of the Navy.

Paul Stillwell: So he apparently changed it at some point.

Mr. Arbor: Somewhere down the line. I got letters. I think I've got a picture he signed for me when we got our commissions. I got that picture downstairs. But somewhere in that 30-year interval where we couldn't find him, in that transitory period—H-A-R-E changed to H-A-I-R.

I asked him that last week.

Paul Stillwell: And what did he say?

Mr. Arbor: Oh, yes, he sloughed me off.

Paul Stillwell: [Laughter]

Mr. Arbor: I said, "One day I'm going to catch you by yourself. I'm going to make you tell me where you were, what you were doing, and who you were doing it with. [Laughter] He just died laughing. He's trying to make up for lost time. In all communication from birth up until—his discharge from the Navy said H-A-R-E. And then after he dropped out of sight up until his reincarnation, he said, "Jesse, yes, it is."

I said, "They didn't change your Social Security number or your service number, did they? You just changed in the way you spell your name unless you went and got a new one altogether." I said, "One of these days I'm going to catch you by yourself."

Because we were pretty tight—Hair, Baugh, and myself. That was before he went out; this was when we were coming through the class.

Baugh and I went to the same college, only Baugh was a couple of years ahead of me. I said, "You know, you didn't know your way around the city of Chicago. You followed me home every weekend, and now you drop out of sight for 30 years and then you come back in, all dressed up with a new name." I said, "And a widower, too."*
[Unclear section]

Paul Stillwell: That is the same person, isn't it?

Mr. Arbor: Oh, yeah, yeah. All there is is a little less hair—not too much there. Same person, same personable little old fellow he always was.

Paul Stillwell: He has one of the sunniest dispositions of anybody I've ever encountered.

Mr. Arbor: It has always been like that. It has always been that way. There's no difference in that disposition from the way he was when we first met. Amiable, quiet, pleasant, easy to get along with. Anybody who can't get along with Hair just [unclear] get along by themselves.

Paul Stillwell: That's a good way of putting it.

As I heard you describe your experiences on board those minesweepers, it sounds as if that was a very enjoyable period in your life.

Mr. Arbor: Very, very, because in those days sailors—especially for those of us who, after having gotten in the Navy, wanted the privilege of going to sea. And we knew that was the first step toward getting aboard the *Mason*.†

Paul Stillwell: Which you thought you had done.

---

* At the time of this interview, James Hair was divorced, not widowed.
† USS *Mason* (DE-529), an *Evarts*-class destroyer escort, was commissioned 20 March 1944. The ship's officers were white; the enlisted men were black.

Mr. Arbor: Which I thought we had done. And we knew if we got open that door, we would get on battleships, and cruisers, and carriers, and the fleet per se. But the greatest thrill was to get your foot aboard a seagoing vessel and to say, "I've been to sea." That's why Hair would always get to talking with members of the group who had no sea duty: "I had more salt in my socks than you fellows had in your entire naval career." Everybody wanted to be an old salt himself.

Paul Stillwell: Did you literally get to sea in those minesweepers?

Mr. Arbor: Oh, about 50 or 60 miles out in the ocean. Because when I got on that big one, I could go head on with those boys instead of flashing those lights—I forget what the code was then. We were towing it back, but with that Roger, we were going right along with it. I just wanted to cross the ocean, but I didn't want to cross until we—and especially when we were out there in the sleet—in January sweeping those mines in the North Atlantic.

Paul Stillwell: Was your ship used as an escort then for part of the time.

Mr. Arbor: No more than outside the gate and back. Outside that light ship, and when we got to that light ship, we would get out of the way and let the big boys do it. Go down beside the—what we called the fist, that's where the mines lay. Cut that degaussing off, so we wouldn't draw him up there.

Paul Stillwell: One of the real ironies of your experience then is that by becoming an officer, you were not able to go to sea.

Mr. Arbor: That's the worst part about it. That's what gives me such a great pleasure now, to see these boys out there now, from admiral down.

Paul Stillwell: Commanding ships.

Mr. Arbor: Commanding ships.

Actually, when they commissioned us, they didn't any more have an idea what they wanted us to do than that dog. They said, "We've got them. Now what are we going to do with them?"

Paul Stillwell: Did you have any opportunity at all to express a wish or desire?

Mr. Arbor: Unh-uh. Nope, never. The only time I questioned the Navy about anything was what was going to be the status of us after the war was over. They wrote me a nice letter, which I have on file down there, the fact that we would be treated as any other reserve officer if we wished to remain in the Navy. So Nelson was the only one accepted it. Nelson said, "I'm just going to see what they're going to do with me, if they're going to keep me. And what they're going to do with me when they keep me."

Thanks to Mr. Nelson and Baugh, there's a Golden Thirteen. There wouldn't be any Golden Thirteen if it hadn't been Nelson involved.

Paul Stillwell: What is your recollection of how they pulled the group back together?*

Mr. Arbor: [Unclear] Knowing Nelson, you missed.

Paul Stillwell: That's true.

Mr. Arbor: Now, you missed the greatest character of the Golden Thirteen or in the Navy. I wish there was some way I could just adequately and accurately describe Mr. Dennis Nelson II.

Paul Stillwell: Well, I appreciate your efforts to try.

---

* Nelson was instrumental in arranging for the group to meet for a reunion in Oakland, California, in 1977. He died in 1979, before the subsequent reunions were held.

Mr. Arbor: It's impossible. However, when Nelson had finished his—had completed his 20th year, he started thinking about something to get us together again. He ran across Baugh in Boston, or just before he got out of the Navy, and they started talking about it. In Baugh's business, he had a contract in Washington. So while he was down in Washington, he went by to see what they call Secretary Miller then. He was Chief of Naval Operations, something like Admiral Miller, now at the Merchant Marine Academy.[*]

And he said, "That's a nice idea."

And Nelson took off from there. The next thing we knew, he started working with the Naval Recruiting Command. They worked with those people so till they got the ball to rolling. And that's a yearly affair—thanks to Nelson and Baugh.

Paul Stillwell: Who came up with the name?

Mr. Arbor: I would be willing to bet my life it was Nelson. Because it sounds like Nelson to come up with something like that.[†]

Paul Stillwell: Yes.

Mr. Arbor: And the plus one that's added, that's that Baugh—something like Baugh would do.[‡] But the whole idea was put up by Nelson. And reading this book, I wish he had had time to—was living now. I bet he could add a volume. Because he was very, very, very perceptive and one of those guys with—anything he conceived and mulled it over for a while—he tried to put it into action. Now, militarily Nelson was the poorest one in the class. But having come from a military family, he knew he was a little step ahead of us when it come to certain aspects of the Navy—from just hearing. So I'll always be eternally grateful to Nelson. He tickled me when he—I like to tell that story about the answer he gave to the questions. Personnel they sent him, why should the Navy

---

[*] Rear Admiral Floyd H. "Hoss" Miller Jr., USN (Ret.) served from 1982 to 1995 as president of his alma mater, the State University of New York Maritime College. He was never Chief of Naval Operations.
[†] The coining of the term "Golden Thirteen" has been attributed to Captain Edward Sechrest, USN.
[‡] In the Golden Thirteen stationery designed by Baugh, in the center was "13+1." The added one was to honor John Dille, who helped the officer candidates during their training at Great Lakes.

keep him or accept him as a regular naval officer. He took the same letter and returned it: "Is there any reason that you can show me why you shouldn't?" And signed "Dennis Nelson II. And that's all the answer he put on it. It came back through, "Accepted." [Laughter]

Paul Stillwell: What do you recall of him from your time undergoing the training together?

Mr. Arbor: Precise, flashy, exotic—a good name you could use.

Paul Stillwell: Do you remember specific incidents that he did?

Mr. Arbor: One specific thing which is not noteworthy, only to him, was washing that car 365 days a year. And then that day of driving over the main side with that top down in the wintertime when the commanding officer's wife arrived. [Laughter] They said, "That's a no for an ensign." [Laughter]

Paul Stillwell: What about during your time in the classes together?

Mr. Arbor: Well, his forte was history. I think his major was history. So the classroom work was already—we structured it after we found out what the textbooks were. We structured it to suit ourselves since we had—there was Mummy with the master's, Cooper was one; Sam Barnes was one; Pinkney had one. So we weren't worried by any counselors or guidance—Syl White's a lawyer, and so on down the road. So we found out what each one's specialty was in that group. And we got the text and did an outline. If it was navigation, I took over. Naval law, Syl would take over. Everybody had—I don't have a breakdown of what it was. But we found that out in less time than two or three days.

Paul Stillwell: Who came up with that idea of pooling your resources?

Mr. Arbor: Don't make me lie; I don't know. It wasn't Jesse.

Paul Stillwell: Was it, perhaps, just a consensus decision?

Mr. Arbor: It sounds more like that because, see, we didn't know each other. So we asked, "What did you do? What did you do? What did you do?" We got the textbooks sitting all around that long table, and it just evolved, that conversation something like—not, "That's mine" in my recollection. Because I don't remember anybody getting up and saying, "I'm going to take over and do so-and-so," or, "You are in charge, what do you . . . ?" It was more or less a consensus just sitting around, because we didn't have time to plan anything. We got there on a Sunday and a Monday—Saturday or Sunday—Sunday. And I think we started class that Monday or early Tuesday morning.

Paul Stillwell: What kind of uniforms did you wear during the training?

Mr. Arbor: Enlisted first class.

Paul Stillwell: Undress blues?

Mr. Arbor: No, we had the whole dress outfit. We just took the—I took the second class—they made us all first class—whatever we were.

Paul Stillwell: Except Cooper, who was a chief already.

Mr. Arbor: Oh, yeah, yeah. So I just took my second class quartermaster off. It was a right-arm rating uniform. First class, all the rest of us—dress blue and undress. We didn't have time to wear the dress jumper.

Paul Stillwell: So probably undress blues.

Mr. Arbor: I put mine on to go [unclear]. Baugh, myself—all of us put that on our dress, yeah.

I have pictures of it. I had one up there. I put some—we all put them on. I think we had the one that we took before we got that commission. I'm almost sure we did. And if we came ashore, we sure put those first class quartermasters on there. Nelson, and I think Cooper's wife was living up there at that time.* Cooper, Lear, Alves, Sam Barnes. Their wives had moved up to North Chicago. So they didn't come in to see us. Baugh, Hair, and Sublett. They lived in Evanston then. And his mother and father were living up there, and he even got married. My old lady never got mad because I stood up at his wedding. And that left nobody but Baugh wasn't married. Hair wasn't married; I wasn't married. Syl White and Mummy Williams were married, so they lived here. So that's what threw Hair and Baugh and I all—because I was the only one they could hang out with if I went home. They could go and sit up in a chair all night, or if we had all to fit sleep in one bed or whatever it was. If I ate, we were going to eat—that's why we got so tight. All the rest of the boys were married, every one of them. And, after all, Hair and I were the last two to get married.

Paul Stillwell: Phil Barnes was married?

Mr. Arbor: No, no, Big Barnes wasn't married, no. I don't know where Big Barnes went. I never did bring him in because I had a car. Nelson, [unclear] had one, and Syl and Mummy always rode up with me.

Paul Stillwell: What about Pinkney and Alves?

Mr. Arbor: See, Alves's wife lived up there. I don't know where Pinkney was. I never remember his having come to Chicago. I know he didn't ever come with me. Because Martin—I took him back once. I took Martin and his wife back up. But Baugh, Hair, and myself—we were all single then, see. Martin was married; everybody was married,

---

* During the officer training program in early 1944, Margarett Gillespie Cooper was living with her mother and baby daughter in Hamilton, Ohio.

but I don't know about Pinkney. He was an old man, we thought; he was much older than we were. So we just put him up there with Nelson.* We thought Cooper was up there with Nelson. Come to find out later he wasn't; he was just a chief.† We thought chiefs had to be old. [Laughter]

Paul Stillwell: He was made an instant chief.

Mr. Arbor: Umm-hmm. So was Nelson.‡

Paul Stillwell: Yes.
What do you remember about the instructors in the course?

Mr. Arbor: I remember the legal instructor very well. And just—Richmond—I'm trying to think what did Richmond teach.§

Paul Stillwell: He apparently was one of the few black instructors, wasn't he?

Mr. Arbor: Oh, Richmond wasn't black.
I hear from him occasionally now that he's up at Michigan.

Paul Stillwell: There was one called Noble Payton apparently.

Mr. Arbor: No, no. Payton, Payton died.

Paul Stillwell: That's what I heard.

---

* Nelson was born in 1907, so he was 36 years old when he was commissioned.
† Cooper was born in 1916.
‡ Nelson was not a chief petty officer.
§ Lieutenant (junior grade) Paul D. Richmond, USN, graduated from the Naval Academy in December 1941. Because of vision problems he was assigned shore duty at Camp Robert Smalls. He was in charge of devising the curriculum for the black officer candidates. His oral history is in the Naval Institute collection.

Mr. Arbor: Yes, Payton died. What did Payton teach? Payton was the only black instructor we had that I remember. He was in one of the hard sciences; I don't know whether it was math or chemistry. He was in one of the hard sciences, I know that, as I remember. As bad as my memory is now, he could have been a chaplain. [Chuckle] I have it mixed up now.

Paul Stillwell: What sort of attitude or approach did the white instructors take toward the group?

Mr. Arbor: In talking with Richmond, Quants [phonetic]—these are the two I talked to after I left, since then. They said the worst feeling they ever had, when they walked in that room and picked up the muster sheet, they had all our academic qualifications behind us.* They said they didn't know what to do. They said, "What the hell did they send me over here for?" And Quants just had his bachelor's. He had guys that had master's, law degrees, [unclear] teacher.

Every time I go to San Francisco, I call Quants, and he comes right on. He says, "I'm still mad because they sent me over there."

Paul Stillwell: But you didn't have the experience in specific subjects that they were teaching.

Mr. Arbor: Well, that's right. Quants was, I forget, navigation—no, he was teaching quartermaster. Something on navigation. That's what he was teaching.

Paul Stillwell: Did you feel that they were condescending toward you?

Mr. Arbor: No, I felt that they just had a job to do—elementary, high school, or college, teaching. "This is your job and you're prepared for it." I never, and they did not as such. They all knew what they were there for, and most of us didn't. And I must say, the way I

---

* Richmond was born in Detroit, Michigan, on 7 November 1920. He was younger than all the members of the Golden Thirteen.

see it, they all poured out their souls, heart, the best they could under the circumstances. I can't remember one incident I can say that they short-cheated us. If they erred—[unclear] it wasn't that they tried to do something to offset the program. Because I believe every instructor they sent over there had our interests at heart. If not, they sure put on a false face. And I don't know any question that anyone asked—if they didn't answer, they'd say, "I'll bring the answer back here tomorrow." And most of them, turned out they'd have a question-and-answer period. "If you men got some question you want—any question you want to ask, ask. I don't know everything, but together we can find out the answers. At least I can go down and go to the library. You can't. That's the difference." You can't expect anything better than that.

Paul Stillwell: Did you feel that the Navy made a good-faith effort in this training program?

Mr. Arbor: Now that's debatable. If I went in a short period of time, I guess they did, but compared to what's—this is from where I sit. But if they had just put us into the V-12 program—they had another program called the Gene Tunney program.* They had three programs. They isolated us—go in there and see if we could swim. See what I mean?

Paul Stillwell: Oh, exactly. You weren't allowed to compete.

Mr. Arbor: Unh-uh. I might not have made it. But the opportunity I'll never know. But then now it's closer together. And I didn't know that grown men could sit down and condense that amount of work and get the results we did. That was one of the greatest things I think to get that—I don't know what action that is—being placed under distress has a natural tendency to move in the direction to undo that distress. That was the action we were working on.

---

* During World War II, V-12 was a Naval Reserve officer training program in which individuals received naval instruction at the same time they worked toward bachelor's degrees. Lieutenant Commander James J. "Gene" Tunney, USNR, had been the heavyweight boxing champion from 1926 to 1928. During World War II, he was in charge of the Navy's program of athletic instruction.

Paul Stillwell: Did you feel a lot of pressure during that time?

Mr. Arbor: I tell you the only time I began to feel any pressure was after we'd been there about a little over half the program. And I didn't have any idea what I was there for. I just thought I was at another service school. I'd been out of one service school and out of another school. But there were so many suppositions. "If you were going to do—if you were to—if you were an officer, if you were going to be an officer, if you—I just got sick of it. And I—that's the time [unclear] bust the whole thing wide open. "Hang it all," I said, "I'm going to find out what's going on around here."

Paul Stillwell: Did you ever at any point during that training come to realize what it was for?

Mr. Arbor: Not until I called over to Big Barnes's sister, [unclear].* It lifted the veils from off my face.

Paul Stillwell: Did the pressure come on at that point?

Mr. Arbor: Came off. Because I was trying to make some good marks so I could go back to Boston and catch that ship, that cruiser—I mean, that destroyer.

Paul Stillwell: Did you contemplate what would happen if you as a group failed?

Mr. Arbor: Never. Never. I don't think we—after we organized ourselves and found out what was going on, we didn't ever think about failing. None of us. We just said, "Nobody in this group is going to fail." Of course, what I knew and the question would come up about history or naval law or something like that—we had all the books there. If I didn't know, "You're the lawyer, Syl."

---

* In the first interview of this oral history Arbor recalled that Phillip Barnes's sister, while working in the office of the Under Secretary of the Navy, discovered that the men were being trained to be officers and reported that to her brother. Arbor recalled that he didn't know until then why the trainees were there. Other members of the group remembered that they knew from the beginning the purpose of the training.

"Now wait," he said, "This is naval law. I have to go ahead and look this up." Then he'd go look it up and come back and call us all [unclear] and listen to him.

Now I'm trying to—Martin was exceptionally good at math. And those questions on equations, or some type of [unclear], we'd run in and call on old Martin.

George was good analytically. Nelson, historian. Barnes, pretty good little historian.* So we had everything we worked with right there.

Paul Stillwell: That's one advantage you had by being a separate group, that you built a group solidarity and camaraderie.

Mr. Arbor: I mean, and it still holds forth today.

Now, when George went to Scotland he called all of us, asked for our input.† I go out here on the coast to help tell about the Golden 13. [Unclear] I call them, "What must I say? What should be my theme? How should I work it up? If you've got any suggestions for me, I have 30 days before I go. Don't let me make a clown out of [unclear] You've got to help me." We go [unclear] like that.

So we started out as a group. Those of us who are left maintain that same camaraderie, and will. And the vine grows stronger each year.

Paul Stillwell: The thing that other members of the group remember you for from that time is a sense of humor, and keeping a light touch if things got tense or so forth. Was that a conscious effort on your part?

Mr. Arbor: Most of the time, yes. Because sometimes you could get so wrapped up in your work, tensions create—somewhere somebody's got to release that valve and let some of the steam blow off. And they'd ask somebody in the various moods, somebody could always rap on the table and say, "Time. Call everything off and let's go back." We had all of that mixture there. And it worked out sometimes it was just spontaneous, most

---

* Samuel E. Barnes was a member of the Golden Thirteen.
† In the late 1980s George Cooper and his wife Margarett visited the ballistic missile submarine *George Washington Carver* (SSBN-656) at Holy Loch, Scotland. Their host was Commander L. V. Beatty, USN, who commanded the submarine from January 1987 to August 1989. The ship was named in honor of a noted African American scientist.

of the time. The Man Upstairs would just free the reins so that he would just let it click at the most opportune time.

Paul Stillwell: Do you remember the sorts of things that you said or did in those circumstances?

Mr. Arbor: No. No. And after this is over, I won't remember what the hell I said today. [Laughter] That's the way I wish it had happened 42 years ago, but there would have been, maybe some frivolous or hilarious moments. [Chuckle] But we had some fun then. It wasn't all—after all, we were getting paid but we were subhuman. [Laughter]

Paul Stillwell: What was a day's routine like for you?

Mr. Arbor: Get up at, be at chow hall before anybody got there in the morning—other than the cook.*

Paul Stillwell: Why?

Mr. Arbor: Contaminate the others. Then we'd come back, hit the books. Then at 11:00 o'clock, before anybody went to chow, we'd drill down to the chow hall. Get out before the regular chow was served.

Paul Stillwell: This is the regular black enlisted men?

Mr. Arbor: Umm-hmm. Yeah. Then we'd come back and hit the books until about 4:00 o'clock.

Paul Stillwell: This is with the instructors in the classes?

---

* This was the chow hall at Camp Robert Smalls.

Mr. Arbor: Yeah. I mean, the instruction started then. And then after 4:00 o'clock we had to eat before the regular enlisted men got there, and we were through with the instructors for the day. And right back up the stairs and the books again. That's every day.

Paul Stillwell: Did you have inspections and cleaning up of the barracks?

Mr. Arbor: Well, we automatically knew to do that. We did that before we came downstairs from upstairs. That was a must. That was routine, just like washing your teeth.

Paul Stillwell: Now, what was upstairs and downstairs? Was this a two-level arrangement?

Mr. Arbor: Umm-hmm. Yeah. Classes downstairs; we had the entire upstairs.

Paul Stillwell: Was it divided into individual rooms or . . .?

Mr. Arbor: No.

Paul Stillwell: Bunk beds?

Mr. Arbor: Umm-hmm.

Paul Stillwell: So you had eight bunk beds for 16 guys?

Mr. Arbor: No, no, no. We had single cots.

Paul Stillwell: I see.

Mr. Arbor: And your desk and your locker. All down this side was that long chow-like table where we studied the entire wing.

Paul Stillwell: Was this table the focus of your activities in the evenings?

Mr. Arbor: That was where we studied. That was the main thing. You know, it was like a regular old chow hall table.

Paul Stillwell: Right.

Mr. Arbor: That's exactly what it was. Just good for eight on one side and eight on the other. And whoever was holding forth was on the end. By the time you finished your lecture or your demonstration, the next one came. We wanted to be sure everybody in the class knew what was going on.

Paul Stillwell: How would you decide what subject was going to be discussed in what sequence?

Mr. Arbor: Whatever our lesson, our assignment was tomorrow.

Paul Stillwell: So if it was navigation, then you'd take it.

Mr. Arbor: In the crash course, you had every class every day.

Paul Stillwell: So you'd sort of set up a rotation.

Mr. Arbor: Umm-hmm. See we had that crash course class. Every subject we had, we had a class in it that next day. No matter if it was chewing gum, we had a class in that.

Paul Stillwell: [Chuckle] Well, perhaps not that.

Mr. Arbor: So you had to be prepared for any eventuality. And we were.

We didn't have time to go to sleep. Time was no object. We didn't have anything but time. We couldn't go anyplace. So when everybody said, "I understand," then we would get up and slap each other on the back—a little horseplay to break the monotony. Never no time for tennis, baseball, basketball, cards, swimming, golf, or anything. It was all work. The only time we'd get to have—relaxing would be a case of someone cracking a joke to break the monotony.

Paul Stillwell: I can guess who that was.

Mr. Arbor: It was one of the other old boys; it wasn't me. [Laughter]

But looking back in retrospect, I wouldn't have it any other way. One never knows how close one can get to a stranger and it be everlasting.

Paul Stillwell: Well, after a while he's not a stranger.

Mr. Arbor: How quickly it came to pass too.

Just that old answer: we were placed under undue stress. And we were. I often wonder sometimes about the life of those of us who were single. We were just trying to get out to go on liberty. Some of the boys were married. It must have been doubly hard for them. And some of them just had gotten married. I know their minds weren't on celestial navigation. [Laughter]

Paul Stillwell: It had to be, though.

What role did John Dille play for the group?[*]

Mr. Arbor: John Dille was—of course, I never saw too much of—John Dille was, I think, Armstrong's adjutant or something. See, I never did know nothing about the

---

[*] Lieutenant (junior grade) John F. Dille, Jr., USNR, was a battalion commander in the leadership structure at Camp Robert Smalls at Great Lakes in early 1944.

command structure at Great Lakes, because I came in for boot camp and service school on up.

Now, Mummy and Syl White were the only two now that could tell you all the intimacies of John Dille and the group. See, in boot camp you just see your company commander and master-at-arms and the man that let you in the chow hall. You don't see the big boys up at the battalion headquarters.

Paul Stillwell: Well, the others have perceived Dille as somebody who was much more supportive and helpful than the other instructors or officers.

Mr. Arbor: Well, I know that he has been more supportive than anybody in the Navy, even until this day. I asked him the other day, I said, "Jack, what prompted you to get so interested in us."

He said, "Jess, I don't know. It just was an assignment that they gave me, and I got attached to this group. And I haven't been able to detach myself until today." But had it not been for Jack Dille that building wouldn't have been named for us.[*] He tried his best to get a ship named for us. But the ships are named for the dead, so let it alone. I don't want one named for me.

He said, "Then the 13s are just nowhere in the ships' nomenclature or anything like that. You've got to be a place, or one individual, or governor, or president, or senator—but 13? And he and Senator Lugar from Indiana—I got all the correspondence down there.[†] He and [unclear] personally worked on that diligently. He said he just never would name a cargo vessel or something like. No, they wanted a maritime ship. I don't want nothing like that. Name one of those big battleships after Big Jesse.

Paul Stillwell: [Laughter] What are your recollections of that dedication for the center up at Great Lakes?

---

[*] On 5 June 1987, at the Great Lakes Naval Training Center, where the Golden Thirteen received their officer training in 1944, the Navy dedicated a new building named for the group. It is used for the in-processing of new recruits.

[†] Richard G. Lugar, a Republican from Indiana, served in the Senate from 3 January 1977 to 3 January 2013. He had served in the Navy from 1957 to 1960. Dille, who ran a media group based in Elkhart, Indiana, evidently had a connection with Senator Lugar.

Mr. Arbor: Very impressive. Now I haven't been there but once. There's still an organization of the memorabilia we want going in. So that was an assignment that we gave Sublett since he's right there at it and nearby—to go up and see how many of us contributed anything to it.* I gave them my uniform and a picture from boot camp, and, I think my health record or something to be on permanent display. And Hair gave his uniform. But most of them had gotten rid of those old uniforms. I would have that uniform of mine if I could have worn it, but it's so big, I couldn't wear the pants, so I just hung it up in a closet downstairs. And, by George, when they wrote me for it, I went down to see if the moths had eaten it, and they hadn't bothered it. All I had to do was shine up the brass and gold on it, and run it through the cleaners.

Paul Stillwell: You didn't know when you got it that it would be such a historical relic.

Mr. Arbor: No. The only reason why I didn't—now that overcoat—I took that crap off and wore that out. And I have two pairs of pants because when I came out of the service, they were wearing—of course, I put cuffs in it. After trying to buy some clothes—you couldn't buy any clothes when you got out—I made myself a couple pairs of pants. And I know things sitting down, I got too big to wear them. So I just hung it up. I just waited around and I had bought a brown suit, the first thing I bought. I had it. I carried that and that Navy uniform everywhere I went. Three weeks ago, my wife went downstairs and said, "Jesse, why don't you try this suit on?"

I said, "Oh, girl, you know I haven't had that suit on since [unclear], and that's 37 years ago." I put that suit on and it fit me to a T after I had just lost all that weight. I wore that suit down to Atlanta last week. [Laughter]

So now, see, I was going up to ascertain just what they wanted us to do with that insofar as pictures that would be—it's no good unless it's put to use and it's fixed up. I imagine as long as Hazard had still been there, but that's the Navy.† You stay so long,

---

* Frank Ellis Sublett Jr. was a member of the Golden Thirteen. His oral history is in the Naval Institute collection. At the time he lived in Glencoe, Illinois, a suburb north of Chicago.
† Rear Admiral Roberta L. Hazard, USN, served as Commander Great Lakes Naval Training Center, July 1985-August 1987. She was enthusiastic about hosting the dedication ceremony. See the Naval Institute oral history of William Sylvester White.

then you go. She had a program lined out for it, but this new fellow has been up there. [unclear, presumably admiral's name]. I've seen him once since the change of command.

And all the other COs up there, at least two or three times a year we had an occasion to go up and discuss naval recruitment. I had fixed up entrees to two high schools here for him about four years ago, which they'd never had. But this CO, I guess he got his quota in. And I'm not going up there with hat in hand, begging him to let me help him. And I told him so. "If you want me to do something, a specific thing, I'd be glad to help you." And I said, "I'm not coming up here with hat in hand begging to let me work with you." I haven't heard from him since. I've got to go up there next—on the 25th. I've been invited up there by one of the officers up there to some meeting, and he's supposed to be in attendance. If he is, okay; if not, okay. If he don't need me, I don't need him.

Paul Stillwell: Well, one thing I've observed about the Navy's efforts in regard to your training: they kept you isolated, and so forth, but they picked good people to send through the training the first time.

Mr. Arbor: Sometimes I question that, looking at me and a few of the others. Out of 270,000 people Jesse Arbor was picked.* Was that an act of providence? Was fate kind or cruel to me? Or have I justified the one who recommended me?

Paul Stillwell: How have you answered those questions in your own mind?

Mr. Arbor: I can look back over my naval career, and I can truthfully say I look at myself in the mirror that I did the very best I could. I'm not ashamed of anything that I did as an officer or as a sailor. The only thing, I wished I had been a little bit smarter, a little bit wiser, because I was a strictly dedicated sailor, as we all were.

And having been one of the guinea pigs, I'm glad I had the endurance, the stamina, the fortitude, or whatever, to withstand everything imaginable. And it has not

---

* The number of black enlisted personnel in the Navy was around 100,000 when 16 of the men began their training in January 1944.

diminished me one iota. I would go back over it again. After all, it wasn't too rough out here.

Paul Stillwell: I think fate was both kind and cruel to you.

Mr. Arbor: Fate was kind to me, kind to us.

Paul Stillwell: Well, it was cruel in the sense that you did not really get an opportunity to demonstrate your potential as commissioned officers.

Mr. Arbor: It just—life—you didn't start running when you stopped crawling. You had to learn how to walk. That's part of the grow-up process. But look at the ones who came behind us. They strut proudly, and they seem to appreciate us when they run across us. That's my reward.

Paul Stillwell: You made the footsteps for them to follow.

Mr. Arbor: And I just hope that this next generation—these are going on pretty good. Now, where the test comes, these that are going in the Navy now who didn't have the parental background that we had. Some of them don't have the educational background. They might have gone further in school than some of us. But they still don't have the background. I'm talking about the ones that are 16, 17, 18, up to 20 now going into the Navy. What fruit will they bear? They can't get them all to go to Annapolis, because they can't make the grade; they can't cut the mustard. What are you going to do? So I take mine out in what's the matter with these youngsters? I'm not trying to drive a man to anything in the Navy. So the opportunities of going to school prepare for life through the Navy. Or if you want to go in the Army or Air Force, what do you want to do? But first you've got to find out what you want. And the worst thing under the sun to do is try to sell them the Navy. I always hear, "What can you do for me?"

I say, "Not a damn thing that you can't do for yourself if you don't want to." I say, "We don't want no dummy in the first place." I say, "How are your grades in school?"

"Well, I can do—"

"It's not what I can do. It's what have you done?"

I say, "Well, they don't want no dummies or babies in the Navy, man or woman."

I start off with them like that so they can't say, "I thought he told me so-and-so."

"Unh-uh. The Navy will train you their way, but you've got to bring them something to work on." "One thing," I say, "you'll appreciate—" And I say, "Your daddy sitting there will appreciate if you go in one branch of the service, let them kick you around some and teach you how to obey. Because I can see here right now, I'm sitting in your house. You haven't been taught to obey right. I see it in this house."

Old [unclear] sitting back right there and baby sister. They'd be so mad. "Why not run that old man out of the house." I talked to one whose dad had a contract cutting lawns in his block. So he had a kid out there—that was three years ago—finishing high school if he could get to the principal to get him through. So he's fussing at him and talking and so on. He had to come up with something.

So I said, "Is that your son, or brother, or what?"

He said, "That's my son."

I said, "You talk to him like that and he responds in kind?"

He said, "Yeah, but he's scared he won't do well."

I said, "When did you start teaching him—last night?" I said, "I'm sitting here. I'm passing on to you and the wife how you can cut mine."

[Interruption for change of tape]

Paul Stillwell: You were in the midst of a story about talking to a fellow who might come into the Navy.

Mr. Arbor: Oh, not might come in. He's in the Navy now.

Paul Stillwell: I see.

Mr. Arbor: This is his third year. And I didn't realize what help I gave, just sitting on the steps talking to his father. And the son happened to overhear the conversation. And after I told him, I said, "You waited too late to start letting him know who was the father." And then all I said, "You see my grass here?" I said, "It's almost sundown. My son is 30-odd years old. But I told him to come over and cut this grass." About that time my son pulled up.

"Hi, Big Jess." I call Little Jess; he calls me Big Jess. I'm a little late now. He came around and had his son.

I said, "You've been sitting over there. Because when I came home, trying to wait for that kid to make up his mind to cut that lawn and you don't pay him."

I said now, "How are your grades? You talk about his graduation. You're going to give him so-and-so for graduation. You don't promise a kid you're going to give him so-and-so if he obeys. You start here, though. You don't wait until they get up where he is now. He's starting way down here. That's wrong. Tell him, 'Don't do that,' and then show him. Then if you can't get his attention, then you've got to get it the other way. Make him hear. You won't have to be embarrassed about it." So he didn't know that I had been in the Navy.

So somebody came past there who knew him. He said, "Now, there's a boy there wants to get in the Navy. You're sitting by a man that can help him out."

I told him I was [unclear] So I was [unclear]. About 9:00 o'clock that night, he and the boy rang the doorbell and came back. I was sitting right there. I talked with him. I said, "Now if you want to go in the Navy, you've got to change your attitude, number one. Because the Navy don't need you. You need the Navy, or somebody or something. I'm going to talk to you like your father should have talked to you." The man was sitting right in that chair, standing up, and wouldn't talk to me. He was so mad. I said, "I will get you an application blank. I will send a Navy recruiter out here. I'm not going to promise you anything. But," I said, "I'll let you use my name at the recruiting office. If they see anything in you, well and good." I forgot all about it. Week before last, that man came up and knocked on the door, and brought me a letter from that boy. He was in

San Diego. He was going in his fourth year in the Navy, and said, "Tell that man—I don't know his name and I don't know his address, but I know he lived right next door to the man who was cutting the grass, the one he brought in his house that night." He's a second class machinist going on his third year. And he's going to school with his—he's going in his junior year in college, still in the Navy. And he said he's got to go back to sea for 18 months. When he comes out, when he's going to finish—I mean, he's not coming out. He's going to finish college. He said he's going to make a career out of the Navy. He said the next time he's in San Diego, he's going to find out my name and address and he's going to pay my way out there and back. And he went back out there, and they told him my name and address, the skipper of his ship called me. That's the kind of results I like to see.

Paul Stillwell: That's so satisfying when something like that happens.

Mr. Arbor: That's better than anything I could have done. Now, suppose I'd taken the attitude, "The hell with him. That's that man's son, and let him talk." They just caught me in the right mood that night. And I try to stay in the right mood, which is hard. I got two or three kids started. Most kids run into [unclear]. They don't want no gals coming into the Navy. They want 96 pounds, straight-A students, want their naval aviator. Now, why do I want that "You're too little; you're a woman. Hell, we want some men." I was so mad, I didn't know what to do.

Had one wanted submarine duty. I said, "You don't know what you're talking about. Bring me the application, and I'll send you to the recruiting office." I said, "I can't put you in the Navy, but other men can. I'm not going to tell anybody, "I'll put you in the Navy, and two years from now you'll be an admiral." That's the trouble with too many of these guys going over the hill now.* You come on—the recruiting officer's just trying to make his quota. I couldn't dare look anybody in the face and tell him, "I'm going to make you—" I can't make him anything. "I'll give you an opportunity to become something. It's up to you. I'm going to give you the keys to the car, teach you how to drive it. The Navy will teach you how to drive it. It's up to you how far you go."

---

* "Going over the hill" is Navy slang for unauthorized absence.

I told three other boys in now—put in all three at the same time. Two made first class. All of them finished four years and re-upped. One went back to the Philippines and got married, and so they put him out. Had a good friend—all didn't even have to go through BOOST or anything like that.* They said they had enough credits to just go—one time they had problems taking the exam and would study to the end—now they're out at San Diego, about 18 months shore duty; they're going to college now. One was a freshman in college; the other was a sophomore when he went in. So when they come out, they're going to have a master's, return to sea duty, and [unclear]. When I spoke on the *Carl Vinson*, one was yeoman on the other end. He was integral in why the skipper invited me out there.

Those are the kinds of things I appreciate. That's the reward I want. I don't want to be patted on the back, "Oh, you're one of the first class"—nothing. I want to help some of these boys on the street. [Unclear section] and changes the course of a young boy who might otherwise go astray. That's the satisfaction I get out of it.

Paul Stillwell: It's interesting that you, as a group, have become heroes in retrospect, but were certainly not treated that way at the time.

Mr. Arbor: Oh, well, that, that—[unclear]. I tell you the only thing that kind of got me—my ruffles up when we got our commission, Baugh and I went back to the college—I told you about that, didn't I?

Paul Stillwell: Yes.

Mr. Arbor: That's the only thing ruffled my feathers. [Unclear] our last [unclear] for the day. Wanted to know would I go back with him. I told him no. "Arbor, there's not too many of us left." He was in the group that went to school there. He says, "I'm presidemt of the alumni association now."†

---

* BOOST – Navy acronym for Broadened Opportunity for Officer Selection and Training. The program was disestablished in 2009 after being incorporated in the Seaman to Admiral program.
† This is a reference to the college Baugh and Arbor attended, now the University of Arkansas at Pine Bluff.

I said, "That's all right. I'm a paid-up member, too, but I'm not going back." At the time I would have enjoyed it. I had that little blue uniform on with a gold band around my arm. You could have called me over to the student union building and introduced me. I said, "You weren't there." I said, "Lawrence Davis was there. He was the president of the college." We were at college the freshman year the same time, same class, we lived 30 miles apart. He had to have known that two of us out of 13 were from that little college, and we were not recognized.

Paul Stillwell: Well, something shabby the Navy did, too, was not give you more recognition—no ceremony, no chance for wives or girlfriends to be there.

Mr. Arbor: That was hard. But I never thought much about that. But I could see myself after having bumped around on that campus, wearing the president's shoes when he wasn't looking. And wearing one pair of corduroy pants almost two years. Dressed in a Navy uniform and the [unclear] college [unclear] because we worked up in the same circumstances, although he was smarter than I was scholastically. He'd gone on and got his PhD while I was in the service, and running up and down the road doing other things.

Paul Stillwell: How did you react emotionally when it came time for you to be commissioned?

Mr. Arbor: The full impact didn't hit me until I got to eat at [unclear]. And what made it so forceful, they never would at Great Lakes. So Hair and Cooper, with fellows like that could go over to the base and get uniforms. They were meek little buzzards. So Baugh and I came down to Finchley's there on Jackson Boulevard and took that little $78.00, $68.00, something they paid for uniforms—they gave us the money. We went down there and got us [unclear] because we had to have tonight, or should have had it yesterday. But we were down there today. So the guy was so pleased to see it. They read about it in the paper. Didn't have the slightest idea they would get any business out of it. Well, that was far away from the naval base up there. So they called a tailor back—he was fixing to go out about 4:00 o'clock. [Unclear] He came back and sewed that gold braid on there and cuffed it—didn't have to do anything with the coats—and stood up there and talked with us and talked to us. He didn't let us have it for $60.00—I think he charged us, oh, $72.00 or $70.00—between $70.00 and $75.00 a suit. Ordinarily it would have been $150.00 suits.

Paul Stillwell: Very nice bargain.

Mr. Arbor: But that in itself was just a part of the awakening to the fact that I was an officer when I got that uniform. Now it didn't bother me so much when he—no, we hadn't been given the commission. But I'd seen that it had been okayed to get the uniform. So I didn't even come out home; of course, I wanted to come home with that uniform on. Then when I—no, we sat there right in that store; I think it was on the 15th floor. So when the tailor started out, he came back—an Italian fellow—he said, "You know what?" He said, "I wouldn't be doing this for my son, this late in the day. But you fellows will be more like my son. I feel proud of you." Everywhere we went—we had our little caps under our arms in a bag. We had the little white hats on, enlisted man's uniform when we went down there.

He said, "I want a picture of you." And when the *Life* magazine came out, it came out with our picture.* And he didn't know [unclear]. I tried to get one to take down there to him, but every time I'd get my hands on one, a relative, or brother, or sister—you just get so many of those Navy ones. I would try to get one to take down there to him and tried to get Baugh to take one. But Baugh said, "You know I'm with all these folks like that." I understood that, but inasmuch as he—not to the manager of the store. The tailor's the one I wanted to give the picture, because he saved me. He just stood up and padded all this, fitted it down, just like he's going to get a $1,000.00 sale out of us. "I'll be more proud of you. You be for yourself," he said. I just—things like that have a tendency to lift one's spirit higher than normally it would be.

Paul Stillwell: This was the Italian tailor?

---

* "First Negro Ensigns," *Life*, 24 April 1944, page 44.

Mr. Arbor: Yeah.

Paul Stillwell: That was such a contrast from the treatment you received from so many other people.

Mr. Arbor: Yeah, especially when one should have received it. Walk in and Armstrong says, "Now how did you get here?"

And I can't bite you back. "Haven't got your orders yet." You got orders in your hand. You got my commission. Now I'm trying to accept it, and you want to know how did I get here? And the way you said it. That's the killing part. Now you got to stand at attention.

Paul Stillwell: Did you have the uniform on, the ensign's uniform to take the oath?

Mr. Arbor: Take what oath?

Paul Stillwell: Didn't you take an oath as an officer?

Mr. Arbor: I didn't.

Paul Stillwell: That's a standard thing.

Mr. Arbor: I didn't.

Paul Stillwell: He just handed it to you?

Mr. Arbor: Just handed it to me. Wasn't nobody in the office but him. Called us in one by one. That's how I got mine. I don't know what he did to the rest of them.

Paul Stillwell: I'm surprised that he didn't also ask you to raise your hand and give you an oath.

Mr. Arbor: Hand raised, nothing. Orders came signed by Secretary of the Navy Knox for the President of the United States.*

Paul Stillwell: But you had the ensign's uniform when you got the commission?

Mr. Arbor: Umm-hmm.

Paul Stillwell: Well, how did the picture come about then that was in *Life* magazine?

Mr. Arbor: *Life*—the first one came out taken was Pathé News. They used to have all the displays, and it was put like a commercial on movie screens in all the theaters.

Paul Stillwell: Newsreels.

Mr. Arbor: Newsreels.

They were the first to come out, and when they missed Syl, they were gone.† *Life* was next in line so *Life* did all—every news plant was out there with cameras. The first day we got our uniform, I ran up to, oh, Dille or Richmond. And we'd been down to the hall to eat breakfast—in fact, I went to the mess hall, ate breakfast and came back, sitting down. We didn't know what to do. We was waiting on Pinkney and Mummy Williams. We don't know where they are. We all get the orders the same time.

Paul Stillwell: You mean that late in the experience you still expected them to get commissioned?

Mr. Arbor: Well, they—let me see—I don't know who got theirs first. I know Cooper was the first one to get his uniform. But they didn't come out just like they call the muster. "Arbor, Baugh, bom, bom, bom, bom . . . here's your orders for your uniform.

---

* Frank Knox (1874-1944) was publisher of the *Chicago Daily News* when made Secretary of the Navy in 1940. He was recalcitrant about bringing black sailors and officers into the Navy. Knox died in office 28 April 1944, just over a month after the Golden 13 were commissioned.
† The first group photo of the officers included only 12 of the 13 because Ensign William Sylvester White had a dental appointment when the shot was taken.

You're officers," something to that effect. I don't know—they would send over a messenger or someone—call them up. No, they didn't call me to the office. I don't know how I got the word to go pick up that uniform, over to the small stores.* Baugh, myself—of course, Hair, and Cooper had already been over there. They could get theirs. So about 9:00 o'clock that morning we went over there, they said, "We don't have anything to fit you." We came went right on back and got leave to come into Chicago. I jumped into old Betsy, and we went down to the Loop in less time than 20 minutes, it looked like. Went up to Finchley's. The man says, "Both of you are lucky. I think both—I know one of you is lucky, because you look like you're about my size, both of you. I was a little bit larger than Baugh. "Ignore that," he said. "I had to sew it myself." Baugh said, "Oh, Lord, Arbor don't let them make you go anywhere else. I may pull out too."

I already told him, I said, "If I can catch this tailor back here before he leaves."

I said, "That's all right. We'll take it up to Great Lakes and have them stripe it. But we couldn't have it done this evening."

So we stepped in the next morning, and they found out we had the uniform. And Cooper and Hair had had theirs a day or two before I got mine and Baugh, as I remember. Because we were the last ones to get the uniform. I'm just trying to reproduce it as nearly as I can remember. And that next morning was the first time any picture was made. So Dille or Richmond came running up topside while we were sitting around the table, waiting on while Pinkney and Alves because Lear had gotten his.

"Why don't you fellows fall out now? Line up and come down." We came down, and they had cameras all over. Everywhere.

"What we want you to do, go by two by two, two go this way—I'm going to stand behind the camera. Two go this way; two go this way." That's the way the first picture was made. We drilled up and down. Back there we stood up, sat down—hats on, hats off. Then they took us over to the gym where they had high steps. Took pictures all that morning. And come to find out Sylvester wasn't there. He had to come downtown to get

---

* Small stores was a uniform shop on the Great Lakes Navy base. Some of the 13 bought their uniforms there; others, including Arbor, got theirs at Finchley's clothing store in Chicago.

his teeth fixed, and he wasn't in the pictures. And that's why Pathé News wasn't an original picture.

Then they had us come back, and they gave us all leave papers. No, no, next morning we went over to pick up—during the commissions.

Paul Stillwell: So the pictures were taken before you got commissioned?

Mr. Arbor: Umm-hmm.

Went over to pick up the leave papers. And after commission, we took off. And, as I recall, I think they gave us ten days—ten or twelve, something like that.

Came back, my orders were on the desk along with Lear's when we got back. Got back on a Monday and left out Tuesday morning for San Francisco.

I was supposed to have flown out, and Lear was supposed to ride the train. I was supposed to stay in Frisco until he got there. So I'd never been in no plane before. I asked the warrant officer there, a yeoman, I said, "I see these orders read the same excepting one thing. I'm to fly to Frisco and wait for Lear to ride out on a train, and we both fly from San Francisco to Honolulu. I said, "What's the rush?" I said, "We're going to the same place, going together." I said, "Hell, I'll be dead two or three days before he gets there waiting for him." [Laughter]

He said, "That is right, Ensign, so he could cut orders on the post at that time."

I said, "Cut me one to ride the train out there. I don't want to get up in that plane anyway." [Laughter]

And then when we get up on [unclear] Baugh overseas.

Another incident that tickled me, show you that black people aren't the only ones that are superstitious. [Unclear section] terminal, you had footlockers, bags and they'd been about as far as from here to Jeffrey, which—oh, I had to go about a half mile to get out to catch the [unclear] where we were. So it wasn't hard to see who I was. Lear was real light complected. Wasn't no question who I was when I was there. Every pilot in those planes ready to take off was hoping I would get on their plane. I didn't know that until I got over to Honolulu. So—

Paul Stillwell: Why did they hope that?

Mr. Arbor: Good luck. It's like that rabbit foot or the black cat. [Laughter]

One of those idiosyncrasies. You can laugh as much as you want.

When I got up on that, started up that ramp, they all sighed. It was a relief. All ran to me, shaking my hand. Wasn't no seats. All the cargo was lashed down with a big net. And you were sitting on, like Indians, sitting around playing cards, eating, and like that. And they were—I think it was 11 hours to fly from Frisco in that prop job. And getting over there, I said, "Man, talk about saying a few prayers." I said, "If I ever get down out of here, you won't get me up here anymore." [Laughter]

But, anyway, sign that short snorter.* You got an hour in Honolulu; it was night about, oh, 1:00 o'clock. The captain came back there and put his arms around me and said, "You brought us through there." He started to say, "Oh, you're just a little shavetail. There ain't no dust on this, is there?"†

So the guy said, "Didn't you read the paper?"

He said, "No, they pulled the paper up, and he wanted to sit down and talk all night."

I said, "Man, I don't know where I am. I got to follow—someone's out there calling my name and lives there and wants to take me up the BOQ." I said, "I don't know where—I got no business being in this plane." I said, "You're going to take off, and I'm not going any further. He was just a lot of fun. See how camaraderie can build or begin. I got that same short snorter that I started out off.

Paul Stillwell: What sort of access were you given to officers' clubs after you were commissioned?

Mr. Arbor: None here. The first order we got was stay out of officers' clubs. Don't go there. The moment we left here, I saw a few officers [unclear] somebody who hadn't

---

* A short snorter is a bank note, often a dollar bill, signed by people traveling together on a flight. The custom is supposed to bring good luck.
† A "shavetail" is an inexperienced, newly commissioned officer. The term is much more commonly used in the Army than the Navy.

heard about me—someone walking around with those little ensign stripes on and [funny noise]. But that didn't faze me. I'd been accustomed to that. I'd been an officer then almost two weeks, three weeks.

Paul Stillwell: You were probably sort of amused by it.

Mr. Arbor: [Laughter] Yes, I was, any number of times. So I let it all pass. But then you get in those clubs after the news broke. And that went all over the Pacific to the effect that we were in the Navy and how we should be treated, or the consequences thereof. We hit those places that those high-ranking officers, they couldn't afford to come down, or they'd send an orderly or his aide would come over. Very seldom I'd sit back with the little peons. I'd go up there with the big boys in my class where the heavy stuff on. [Laughter] They wanted to know why you were born. Where? Where were your mother and father born? What did they look like? How tall were they? What did you do before you were born? All that—I knew that stuff. Who are you talking to? Captains and admirals and vice admirals, rear admirals. There—everywhere you looked there were pictures of admirals on the wall, you see.

Paul Stillwell: You were a curiosity at that point.

Mr. Arbor: Any place. Now down at NOB in Honolulu you have to pay a quarter for a whiskey, a drink of whiskey.* Just set your glass up—anyway, somebody'd want to buy you a drink and see how you could hold it, whether you can hold it, talk to you, ask you the same damn-fool questions: "Where did you go to school? How far? Why were you born? What for?"—and all them. Anybody in the Navy outranks you; you know that. You just got yours yesterday, and if he got his the day before, he outranks you so you got to salute everybody. Why, we'd been taught that, and that's naval courtesy. So if you're in the ball game, you learn the rules of the game first. You play by the rules, and you won't have any trouble.

---

* NOB – naval operating base.

Paul Stillwell: Did you mind that you were being treated this way by the senior officers?

Mr. Arbor: Yes, to an extent. They didn't call little Joe Palooka about where he'd been.*

Paul Stillwell: Of course they didn't.

Mr. Arbor: Why didn't they call him and ask him those silly questions?

I don't know what this one boy was; he was American, but I'm trying to find out whether he was part Middle East extraction or someplace, light brown complected. But he used to tell me, "Do you know one thing, Ensign?" He said, "You're taking a lot of weight off me."

I said, "What the hell are you talking about?"

He said, "I get so sick of people asking me, 'What am I?'." He said, "They can look at you and tell what you are." [Chuckle]

I said, "Well, I can laugh and cut it off. I can sit and look as sorrowful as the occasion may appear." But then they go through—I got a point where I can set a mental thermostat, a mental block, and everything instead of coming, going to [unclear]

Paul Stillwell: In one ear and out the other.

Mr. Arbor: Out the other. They had to go over and past me. That's where I set my thermostat when I go in with those high-ranking officers. Number one, he puts his pants on one leg at a time, just been doing it longer. He's got a higher rank, and along with that rank goes higher responsibility, greater responsibility. And one of those responsibilities is how you treat your underlings.

Paul Stillwell: Did any of them treat you with dignity?

Mr. Arbor: All of them. All of them but the one that found—he slept under the tent that night, which was against his religion.

---

* Joe Palooka was a comic strip character of the era, a Caucasian boxer.

Paul Stillwell: Well, the ones who were asking the questions, though, were patronizing you.

Mr. Arbor: I know it. And I had sense enough to know that. But I can't blow a fuse. I don't know which one of those buzzards was going to be my CO tomorrow. I got to live with it. As long as he's patronizing, I know what he's doing. Some of them were sincere, and some were inquisitive. But I had to satisfy all of them.

Paul Stillwell: So it varied.

Mr. Arbor: Oh, yeah. But I believe they all were sincere when they looked up and saw me. Now, when the first Marine—he wasn't an officer—that hit our tent in the Pacific—he was a classmate of mine in college. He said of one individual, "That same man who was our commander up there when you got to Guam, was our commander on Guadalcanal. So he came there and stayed about three weeks." And said, "We were the first ones that landed." He said, "There may be another fight," to make shore patrolmen out of them—sentries, anything. And so when—Larson called us up to his headquarters, all of us, the whole company, and welcomed us to the islands. Here's what he said, 'When I came back from down under, I found out they had you people in our Marine Corps, I started to turn around and go back. What the hell is this Marine Corps coming to?'"

Paul Stillwell: This Larson was on Guam?

Mr. Arbor: Umm-hmm. Yes, that's the one that came to Guam. In about three weeks he was gone, and I realized what he had said was that in that time he had the chance to be reborn again. [Laughter] But that was a sincere mistake. That's all he'd been taught. He'd never seen blacks in the Marine Corps. Not even as cooks. They didn't have no black cooks in the Marine Corps. So it was total reconversion to him. In the Navy they did see some cabin boys, stewards, mess attendants, cooks, but in the Marine Corps there was no pretense.

Paul Stillwell: What was your most satisfying experience as a commissioned officer?

Mr. Arbor: It varies.

See, satisfaction comes with performance, satisfactory—I've been most satisfied since I had the uniform off with such instances that I just stated before with those two boys, those three boys, and this one in particular.

Paul Stillwell: Well, I was thinking of that time in the Pacific. Are there any occasions that really stand out for you where you accomplished something that you felt very proud of?

Mr. Arbor: Oh, when I went to, left Honolulu, it was right after an uprising then with the boys and this commander there, Avant.

Paul Stillwell: You told me about the intercession after there had been some mistreatment of people.

Mr. Arbor: Oh, yeah, and getting—that's, that's, I feel, one of my greatest accomplishments. Whenever I think I aided or assisted somebody in overcoming any particular obstacle or reaching some type of a goal, that's what I—I'm not looking for any pat on the back or self-glorification, or anything like that, except I can aid or help somebody. That's what I was sent out there to do. Now I don't want it ever said that I went with hat in hand and didn't live up to an officer's expectations. No more, no less. And that's my yardstick every day. If I had to go back in the Navy tomorrow, I would carry with me the same fundamentals I would—see, the Navy didn't make a man out of me; I was a man when I went in. It just made me a commissioned officer. Yes, I may be a little frivolous at times, which is part of my makeup. It is part of my game plan. Sometimes you have to change a trend of someone's thoughts. They'll get your ideas through sometimes. And I practiced that for a long period of time, so it's almost second nature. And then, too, I didn't have the opportunity to come up with the formal education like the rest of the boys did. I had to learn mine in the alleys and the pool halls. I had to pick it up from those intellectuals that I associated with up there at Robert Smalls—just Judge White and Dr. Barnes, Dr. Cooper.

Paul Stillwell: Well, I think you held your own.

Mr. Arbor: And then I took what little I had and added what I picked up from them and they took me along. That's fair to say. And I'm proud for having known those fellows.

Paul Stillwell: Everybody who was in that group contributed, including you, certainly.

Mr. Arbor: I like to think we all did, in all sincerity. If not, we made a damn good effort.

Paul Stillwell: That's right.

Mr. Arbor: I've never been around a group of boys that nobody looked like had any reason to have animosity toward others. Everything was bent toward helping each other.

I often think what the world would be if all of us in our everyday lives could maintain that same camaraderie. From the President down to the humblest person in the States.

Paul Stillwell: I think one thing that prevents that is that there is too much selfishness, and from what I've heard there was not selfishness in that group.

Mr. Arbor: You know I've often wondered, so many—the various characters there just popped in overnight, and every one of us had a little ego in us; otherwise, they wouldn't have accepted us. They picked us for something, other than intelligence. And for us to submerge all those egos and personalities together overnight. It had to be providential. That's the only thing I can say.

It must have been an act of providence. Now there were too—and if it would have been little children, that would have been different. We were all grown men. Some of us tottering along the ages of old men. [Laughter]

Paul Stillwell: Close to 30.

Mr. Arbor: Yeah, that's an old man. You remember when you were 14 or 15 years old, man, 40 years old. That's your granddaddy.

Some of us were worrying 30 to death, and I think Nelson was one of them. I know he was the senior citizen.

I had a card from her the other day. I sent her a—

Paul Stillwell: Mrs. Nelson?

Mr. Arbor: Umm-hmm. I sent her a cassette of the in-processing and graduation ceremony. I had the two and spliced them. I did a little editing. so I'd get both the main parts of the graduation in and much of the in-processing that I could. I thought the least I could do for her since Dennis's death. And I sent Baugh's wife one. Those two boys—they are—they were the beginning of this Golden Thirteen and its successes all the way down to then. Because God knows none of us would have done a damn thing toward that end. Not one of us. Regardless who said they did anything. I am here to say not one of us from Dennis Nelson, the originator, and Dalton Baugh, the activator.

That stationery we write on, that's Dalton Baugh's idea. And his wife told me the other day one morning she found the printing plate. If we run out, she found the plate.

So we should always be eternally grateful, even to the last one of us, when we reach up and get our hats, we should write Nelson's wife, and Baugh's wife, telling when I'm going to join them. Let them know I still appreciate the efforts they took getting us back together. I can be no greater compliment for a friend.

That's the way I feel toward all of them but specifically Baugh and Nelson, because they were men of action. All of us could give you some grandiose ideas that would knock the top your head off, but you better hold our feet to the fire. Nelson would start shaking his head and walking, and he'd worry the hell out of you until you do something to get rid of him. And Baugh was so quiet and nice and professional. Tell you to do something, keep nice quiet, soft voice. And talking softly, and to the point always.

All business and his business reflected it too. But my man would always be Nelson. [chuckle] He was the closest thing—we were the closest thing to each other. [Laughter]

Paul Stillwell: Well, unless you have anything to add, I think that's a very good note to end on.

Mr. Arbor: I'm sorry I couldn't have been of any greater service to you.

Paul Stillwell: You have done a very great service, and I thank you.

Mr. Arbor: Glad to have had the opportunity to add what little bit I could—had it only been done, as I said in the previous tape, at least 40 years ago.

Paul Stillwell: We do it when we can, and I'm glad we've done it now.

Mr. Arbor: Thank you.

Index to the Oral History of
Mr. Jesse W. Arbor, Member of the Golden Thirteen

Alcohol
    Freely available to naval officers who served in the Pacific during World War II, 15
    Arbor demonstrated a great ability to hold his liquor while on Guam in World War II, 65-66

Alves, A.
    Played basketball in school before joining the Navy, 92-93
    Black petty officer who went through officer training with the Golden Thirteen at Great Lakes in 1944 but was not commissioned, 12-13, 60, 92, 130, 152

Arbor, Jesse W.
    Grandparents were born in slavery, 33-34, 36
    Parents, 1, 29-39, 51, 84-85, 99
    Siblings, 1, 30-32, 37-39, 97
    Wife Autry, 107, 141
    Children, 36, 81-84, 107-108, 145
    Grandchildren, 81-82
    Growing-up years and education in Cotton Plant, Arkansas, in the 1910s and 1920s, 29-36, 84-85
    Attended college and played football in Arkansas in the 1930s, 8-9, 13-14, 38, 47-50
    In the 1930s worked as a Pullman porter on railroads, 40-41, 45-47, 51-52, 69-70, 74, 113
    Lived and worked in Chicago in the 1930s until he entered the Navy in 1942, 1-2, 31, 37-41, 69-91
    In 1940 read speeches in Chicago on behalf of possibly dubious groups, 71-75
    Enlisted in the Navy in September 1942 to avoid being drafted into the Army, 1-3,
    Recruit training and service school at Great Lakes, Illinois, Naval Training Station in 1942-43, 3, 52-57, 77-79, 95-97
    Based in Boston on board two ships in 1943, 3-6, 57-58, 99-112
    Received officer training at Great Lakes, January-March 1944, 4-13, 60-62, 119-143, 148-150, 158-159
    First assignment as an officer was to Pearl Harbor in 1944, 14-15, 27, 56, 66-68, 79-80, 115-119, 153-158
    During the latter part of World War II was stationed on Guam, 15-21, 63-66, 113-114, 157
    Inquired about staying in the Navy after the end of World War II but decided not to, 20-22
    Except for his time in the Navy, ran a clothing and dry cleaning business in Chicago from the early 1940s to the late 1960s, 21, 41-42
    From 1968 to 1984, worked as a boiler engineer in a Chicago school, 42-45
    In his later years advised prospects for military service and helped with recruiting, 81-84, 143-147

Arkansas Agricultural, Mechanical and Normal (AM&N) College, Pine Bluff
　　In the 1930s Arbor and fellow Golden Thirteen member Dalton Baugh attended the school, 8-9, 13-14, 38, 45, 47-50, 86-89, 147-148

Armstrong, Commander Daniel W., USNR (USNA, 1915)
　　Served as officer in charge of Camp Robert Smalls at Great Lakes, Illinois, in early 1944, 10, 12-13, 27-28, 119-120, 150
　　Later served at Pearl Harbor, 27

Army, U.S.
　　Arbor's uncle served in the Army in World War I, 32-33
　　Arbor's relatives convinced him not to go into the Army in World War II, 1

Avant, Lieutenant Commander Grady, USNR
　　While stationed at Pearl Harbor in World War II, was Arbor's commanding officer and made a racial slur during a poker game, 66-68, 115-119, 158

Bamford, Lieutenant (junior grade) Robert T. Bamford, USN (Ret.)
　　While stationed in Boston in early 1944, advised Arbor about the officer training program, 10-11, 57-58

Barnes, Phillip G.
　　Member of the Golden Thirteen who underwent officer training at Great Lakes, Illinois, in early 1944, 9-12, 92, 130, 134
　　His sister, who worked in Washington, D.C., provided information on the training program, 9-10

Barnes, Samuel E.
　　Member of the Golden Thirteen who underwent officer training at Great Lakes in the early 1944, 9-10

Baugh, Dalton L.
　　Attended a small black college in Arkansas before joining the Navy, 13-14, 45, 124, 147-148
　　Service in a Boston-based minesweeper in World War II as an enlisted man, 109
　　Member of the Golden Thirteen who had a hand in getting the group back together in 1977 and made up special stationery to honor the group, 12-13, 121-122, 126, 160
　　Was close with Arbor during the officer training period in 1944, 124, 130, 151-152, 160

Boston, Massachusetts
　　Arbor was based there in 1943 while serving on board two ships and attending navigation school at Harvard, 3-6, 99-112

Camp Robert Smalls
Site of training for black enlisted men and the first black officer candidates at Great Lakes, Illinois, in early 1944, 3-13, 22, 27, 52-57, 60-62, 77-79, 95-97, 119-143, 148-150, 158-159

White entertainers were given priority over talented black professional performers, 94-95

Carl Vinson, USS (CVN-70)
In 1986 Arbor made a talk on board this aircraft carrier about his Golden Thirteen experiences, 25-26, 59

Chicago, Illinois
Minimal recognition for Jean du Sable, who settled in what became Chicago in 1779, 28-29

This city was Arbor's home base from 1930 onward, 1-3, 20-22, 28, 31, 37-50, 69-71

In 1939, Arbor recalled, he had a tryout with the Chicago Cardinals of the National Football League, 50-51

In the late 1930s-early 1940s Arbor worked at the Chicago Beach Hotel, 39-40

Atmosphere for servicemen in World War II, 104

Arbor lived and worked in the city after being released from the Navy after World War II, 21, 41-45, 81-84, 143-147

Chicago Defender
In the 1930s Arbor's football exploits were covered in this black newspaper, 38, 86

Cooper, George C.
Member of the Golden Thirteen who was a chief petty officer during training, later the first of the group to wear an officer's uniform, 11-12, 128, 130-131, 135, 151-152

Saved documentary material about the Golden Thirteen, 27-28

In the late 1980s Cooper and his wife visited the ballistic missile submarine *George Washington Carver* (SSBN-656), based in Holy Loch, Scotland, 135

Dille, Lieutenant John F., Jr., USNR
Reserve officer who provided valuable moral support when the members of the Golden Thirteen were undergoing officer training at Great Lakes, Illinois, in early 1944, 59, 139-140, 151-152

Had a role in getting a building at the Great Lakes Naval Training Center, named for the Golden Thirteen, built and commissioned in 1987, 140

Draft
Until the middle of World War II, individuals entered the Navy as volunteers, then as draftees thereafter, 25, 93-94, 100

Du Sable, Jean Baptiste Pointe
    In 1779 settled in what is now Chicago and was later recognized as its founder, 29

Enlisted Personnel
    In June 1942 the Navy began accepting blacks in general service ratings, 26
    Crew members of the minesweeper *Hawk* (AM-133) and auxiliary *Guinevere* (IX-67) in 1943, 99-1121
    In early 1944 enlisted Navy men were trained at Great Lakes, Illinois, to become the Navy's first black line officers, the Golden Thirteen, 4-10, 27, 61-62, 92, 119-140, 142, 146-150, 158-159

Federal Bureau of Investigation
    In the early 1940s investigated the backgrounds of black men who were potential Navy officer candidates, 71-72, 75-76

Football
    In the 1930s Arbor played right tackle for Arkansas Agricultural, Mechanical and Normal (AM&N) College, Pine Bluff, 38, 49-50, 86-89
    In 1939, Arbor recalled, he had a tryout with the Chicago Cardinals of the National Football League, 50, 88-91
    Several of the members of the Golden Thirteen had played football before entering the Navy, 92-94

Gambling
    While stationed at Pearl Harbor in World War II, Arbor's commanding officer made a racial slur during a poker game, 66-68, 115-119, 158

Golden Thirteen
    Enlisted Navy men who were trained at Great Lakes, Illinois, in early 1944 to become the Navy's first black line officers, 4-10, 27, 60-62, 92, 119-143, 146-150, 158-159
    Several of the members of the Golden Thirteen had played football before entering the Navy, 92-94
    In March 1944 the 13 men were commissioned individually with no graduation event after passing the course of study, 11-13, 150
    Not allowed to use the BOQ or officers' club at Great Lakes after commissioning, 13, 154
    A building at the Great Lakes Naval Training Center, named in honor of the Golden Thirteen, was commissioned in 1987, 140-141

Great Lakes, Illinois, Naval Training Station
    Site of boot camp and service school for Arbor in 1942-43, 3, 52-57, 77-79
    Site of officer training for the Golden Thirteen in early 1944, 4-10, 27, 60-62, 119-143, 146-150, 158-159
    Members of the Golden Thirteen were not allowed to use the BOQ or officers' club at Great Lakes after commissioning, 13, 154

Commander Donald G. Gumz commanded Camp Robert Smalls late in World War II, 22

A building at the Great Lakes Naval Training Center, named in honor of the Golden Thirteen, was commissioned in 1987, 140-141

Guam, Mariana Islands
In the latter part of the war Golden Thirteen members Jesse Arbor and Charles Lear were stationed on the island, 16-20, 63-68, 113-114, 157

A white officer was upset when he learned that he and Arbor had slept in the same BOQ one night, 114-115

***Guinevere*, USS (IX-67)**
Boston-based auxiliary schooner in which Arbor served in 1943, 4, 110-112, 125

Gumz, Commander Donald G., USN (USNA, 1936)
Late in World War II served as officer in charge of Camp Robert Smalls at Great Lakes, 22

Hair, James E.
Member of the Golden Thirteen who attended Bethune-Cookman College and Xavier University in the 1930s, 92

Was close with Arbor during the officer training period in 1944, 124, 130, 152

Confusion over the spelling of his last name, which was H-A-R-E during his time in the Navy, 122-124

***Hawk*, USS (AM-133)**
Boston-based minesweeper in which Arbor served in 1943, largely black crew, 4, 99-109, 112, 124-125

Hazard, Rear Admiral Roberta L., USN
As Commander Great Lakes Naval Training Center, presided at the 1987 dedication of an in-processing center named in honor of the Golden Thirteen, 141-142

Hope, Lieutenant Commander Edward S., Civil Engineer Corps, USNR
Highest-ranking black officer to serve in the U.S. Navy during World War II, 19

***Kidd*, USS (DDG-993)**
Guided missile destroyer that served as the site of a Golden Thirteen reunion in April 1982, 59

Lear, Charles B.
Member of the Golden Thirteen who was made a warrant boatswain in 1944, 14, 152

First assignment as an officer was to Pearl Harbor in 1944, 14-15, 153

During the latter part of World War II was stationed on Guam, 15-16, 113

Leave and Liberty
In 1943, while based in Boston, Arbor seldom went on liberty with white shipmates, 112

Lehman, John F. Jr.
As Secretary of the Navy in the 1980s attended a convention of the National Naval Officers Association (NNOA), 24

***Life* Magazine**
When members of the Golden Thirteen were commissioned in March 1944 they were featured in a newsreel and *Life*, 11, 149, 151

Marine Corps, U.S.
Compared with the other services, the Marines were latecomers to accepting black personnel in World War II, 157

Martin, Graham E.
Member of the Golden Thirteen who went through officer training at Great Lakes, Illinois, in early 1944, 130, 135

***Mason*, USS (DE-529)**
Destroyer escort to which Arbor was initially assigned before he received orders to officer training in 1944, 4-5, 58, 124

Medical Conditions
In 1945 Lieutenant (junior grade) Jesse Arbor used an allergy to citrus fruits to keep from going back to the Western Pacific, 20-21

National Naval Officers Association (NNOA)
At annual conventions of NNOA in the 1980s Arbor counseled serving black naval officers about career potential, 23-25

Nelson, Dennis D. II
Flamboyant member of the Golden Thirteen who went through officer training at Great Lakes, Illinois, in 1944, 7, 11-13, 22, 128, 131
After World War II received a regular Navy commission, the only one of the 13 who stayed for a full career, 22, 126-128
In 1951 wrote a book on the racial integration of the Navy, 26, 122
In 1977 joined with Dalton Baugh in getting the Golden Thirteen together again, 127, 160-161

News Media
In the 1930s Arbor's football exploits were covered in the *Chicago Defender*, a black newspaper, 38, 86

When members of the Golden Thirteen were commissioned in March 1944 they were featured in a newsreel and *Life* magazine, but most coverage was in the black press, 11, 149, 151-153

Pearl Harbor (Hawaii) Naval Base/Naval Station
In 1944 Jesse Arbor and Charles Lear became the first two black officers assigned to Pearl Harbor, 14-15, 56, 79-80, 115-119, 153-158
While stationed at Pearl Harbor, Arbor's commanding officer made a racial slur during a poker game, 66-68, 115-119, 158

Pinkney, J. B.
Black petty officer who went through officer training with the Golden Thirteen at Great Lakes in 1944 but was not commissioned, 12-13, 60, 121, 131, 151-152

Port Chicago, California
Site of an ammunition explosion in July 1944 that killed many black sailors, 105-106

Racial Issues
Arbor had no racial problems growing up in Arkansas in the 1910s and 1920s because his home county's citizens were almost all black, 34
At Camp Robert Smalls in World War II, white performers were given priority over talented black professional performers, 94-95
In 1943, while based in Boston, Arbor seldom went on liberty with white shipmates, 112
Members of the Golden Thirteen were not allowed to use the BOQ or officers' club at Great Lakes after their 1944 commissioning, 13, 154
In 1945 a lieutenant commander in Pearl Harbor issued a memo saying that black officers were to be treated the same as their white counterparts, 14
A white officer was upset when he learned that he and Arbor had slept in the same BOQ on Guam one night late in the war, 114-115
Compared with the other services, the Marines were latecomers to accepting black personnel in World War II, 157
Following the Golden Thirteen commissioning in March 1944, the Navy commissioned dozens more black officers later in the war, 18-19

Recruiting
A recruiter enlisted Arbor in the Navy in September 1942, 1-3
In his later years Arbor advised prospects for military service and helped with recruiting, 81-84, 143-147

Religion
Role in the Arbor family from the 1910s to the 1930s, 85

Richmond, Lieutenant (junior grade) Paul D., USNR (USNA, 1942)
Reserve officer who supervised the curriculum for the training of the Golden Thirteen at Great Lakes, Illinois, in early 1944, 131-132, 151-152

Sublett, Frank E. Jr.
　　Member of the Golden Thirteen who had been at service school in Hampton, Virginia prior to the group's during training period at Great Lakes, Illinois, in early 1944, 4, 7, 9
　　Overseeing Golden Thirteen memorabilia at the building at Great Lakes named for the group, 140-141

Uniforms-Naval
　　In 1944 members of the Golden Thirteen wore enlisted Navy uniforms during their training and then bought officer uniforms shortly before they were commissioned in March, 11, 129-130, 148-152
　　Members of the group have donated their old uniforms to the building at Great Lakes that honors the Golden Thirteen, 141

White, William Sylvester
　　Member of the Golden Thirteen who earned a law degree before undergoing training at Great Lakes, Illinois, in early 1944, 61, 92, 130, 134-135, 140, 151-153

Williams, Lewis R.
　　Black Navy enlisted man who went through training with the Golden Thirteen in 1944 but was not commissioned as an officer, 12-13, 59, 69, 92, 120, 128, 130, 140, 151

www.ingramcontent.com/pod-product-compliance
Lightning Source LLC
Chambersburg PA
CBHW080612170426
43209CB00007B/1411